tomorrow is another song

tomorrow is

another song

scott wannberg

Perceval Press

3 new voices,

dustin holland
nick martinson
mj taylor

They keep me aware and awake.

tomorrow is another song
scott wannberg

ISBN 0-9819747-7-5
Copyright 2011 Perceval Press

Perceval Press
1223 Wilshire Blvd., Suite F
Santa Monica, CA 90403
www.percevalpress.com

Editors:
Henry Mortensen
Viggo Mortensen

Copy Editor:
Sherri Schottlaender

Design:
Michele Perez

Cover Photo:
Viggo Mortensen, *Frontera, junio* (2009)

Printed in Spain at Gráficas Jomagar S.L.

Contents

this house claims nobody's home

one last round

In the corner of the kitchen where bad children have to sit facing the wall with soap scraped against their teeth, a ray of sunshine shines down on each and every one of them, offering hope. As long as you can find great art, there is hope. Great artists help us find meaning in the chaos of society, politics, sex, and religion. This is why Scott's writing spins me into another dimension. The way Scott takes the world apart and puts it back together is magical. He is the word sorcerer, renaming nouns, shuffling vowels, and turning it all into one long, hyphenated construct of beautiful new meaning. I have seen him, numerous times, start talking and spontaneously pull this off, live and in person. This is an experience not to be missed. The sun is beaming and hiding behind clouds, and Scott is somewhere in Oregon. We miss him here in Southern California, but here's a book you can treasure, like Grimm's Fairy Tales, Eastern philosophy, or a Golden Book. In his intricate way, Scott has simplified and explained and taught and saved. Whenever I read Scott's poems, I hear his voice. I see his face, his stature. I feel his presence. He is love and peace and goodness. He is a warrior for our side, and I honor him.

Exene Cervenka

I really miss seeing Scott at Dutton's in Brentwood. He's the best-read man I ever met, and a cinephile to boot. If I was inside Scott's head I don't think I could stand it. The guy's brain is on fire. Flip this book open to any one of the poems in this collection and find a treasure. The man can't stop:

I figured I'd just keep walking
until the earth fell asleep

He uses words like the great painters paint: flinging, dripping, looping, splattering like Pollock or laying them out with the intense humor, vitality, and disregard for convention of Dubuffet. The analogies could go on and on. Scott gets behind the center and calls audibles like Peyton Manning, riffs like Bird and Miles, and hits the highs and lows like Yma Sumac. His poetry can be political, polemical, personal, and provocative, and he shies away from cheap alliteration. His work is contemporary and timeless, brave and honest, and fun as hell to read.

Raise your hand
if you remember the ancient days
of the heart:
how it once held court,
how it once led our chorus.

Scott remembers the ancient days of yesteryear and won't let us forget tomorrow. Enjoy.

Ed Harris

there's this old story . . .

There's This Old Story . . .

There's an old story that begins,
don't trust the storyteller.
Don't know how it winds up,
somewhere during the middle,
the ceiling split some.
Obnoxious air got in.
Kind of difficult to glib palaver.
Wake me up when the killer gets unmasked.
Tell them at the mountaintop they really don't need to wait for me.

There's this old movie that begins,
don't believe everything you see.
Don't know how it resolves,
the heart torn up some.
Irrefutable pain wafted in.
I like the music you brought.
Go on, put something up.
None of us truly go all that far,
no matter how long and hard we run.

There's this old man,
he swears he's a young woman.
Don't know what room he'll sleep it off in.
The world hasn't a clue,
leave it at that.
Tell the dour carny barkers
to save their schtick for
another
day.

Atom Bomb Boogie

Man mounted a crazy horse.
Take me to your leader, he said.
All the crazy horses had recently disowned leaders.
They firmly believed in impulse.
Impulse called me up way too early.
I'll be over soon with something magical.
I thought all things magical have been extradited.

There's an ongoing hole in the middle of the street.
Sometimes it goes wide.
Sometimes it runs deep.
You could put various symphony orchestras in it.
The atom bomb needed a place for the night,
hopefully not too close to the busy freeway.
There are believers in the Cracker Jack box.
A government woke up in the psycho ward.
What am I? it felt.

There's a long line of loveable losers
trying to keep from getting burned by the sun.
I sit down with zombies and men who do what they must.
We talk about the old sleight of hand
Ponzi schemes on ice.
How the world is a thrift store
needing to pay its rent.

They put Mickey Rooney and Judy Garland on the new stimulus bill.
One glistening hammer and a city jail full of nails.
Gonna build it to last, ladies and gents.
The *Titanic* gets a rematch with that iceberg.
I got a hootenanny in my flat feet.
I got my last-will-and-testament coloring book.
Tonight we rise to the occasion.
Preheat the oven at 350.

Man ran around in circles.
He claimed the investigation was officially closed.
All the drinking whiskey runs for office.

The lovers wear bulletproof vests.
The river wants to take a hot bath.
The ghosts finally form a union.
The worn-out wallpaper skin of my heart
just struck it rich.

Gonna make you want to learn to soar.
Gonna make you Technicolor.
Black and white and I
go shopping.
The shelves might be empty
but the music they pipe in will kill you.

Gonna Lay Down the Law

Gonna lay down the law on your ass,
he claimed,
then lit himself on fire.
His latest flame threw holy water on him.
He thanked her profusely,
yanked her ponytail,
made her wince.
I love you, he crooned,
but I gotta lay down the law on your ass.
You might think you don't need it,
but I know different.
I've slept on incorrigible back roads.
I've starved at the feasts of plenty.
In some lost fool's valley
I saw argumentative stars in the sky.
Sometimes I might give you a little bit of pain.
What comes around goes out the other end.
She shrugs when he gets this way.
She's heard his book of prayer way too long.
You won't mangle my song, she sang.
My ears quit working days ago, he replies.
When they get going like this,
it makes me want to turn into a rock.
Toss me into the dark,
let me fall where I'll never know.
Gonna plant my flag, he swears,
Gonna make the world sit up and pay heed.
The flies all move into his hair.
Maybe we could use some comic relief.
The Earth quakes when he finishes a sentence.
With connections like that
a guy could go places.

Some Sundays

Got to get off your bed, I say,
you can't lay inert, a sponge soaking up
nothing. He hands me a would-be
urinal, says, go empty this.
I can't get off the bed, he says.
You want a book to read? A crossword puzzle?
I know you love crossword puzzles.
Get off your bed, move around.
Never should have tried to take that bath.
His legs wind up under him in such a tortured position,
I will never really know how he got them there.
Uncle Bob is coming over to drive me to the market.
I need to get things to eat.
You need to eat, I tell him.
I want ice water, he says.
I want water with ice.
I run through a lot of ice.
You can't live on ice water, you need to eat.
Got to get off your bed, I say.
His leg swells.
His right leg is in pain.
Same leg they did the procedure on.
Catheter into femoral artery then up to part of liver
where cancer is, zap with chemo,
hopefully reduce cancer enough so surgery can be attempted.
I rub mineral ice on his leg.
Don't know it's a blood clot.
I go out and tell uncle Bob I need his help.
Ernie's fallen.
He wanted to make it to the living room chair
but nothing doing.
He lies there between the beds.
My uncle is helpless.
Ernie, I don't know what to do, he says.
I want to die, my father says, lying on the carpet between the beds.
I don't have anything to make you die, I say,
and get him on the bed.
Uncle Bob calls his doc.

The doc says get him to the ER.
Scott can help you get him in the car.
No go.
Call Schaeffer Ambulance.
They say three and a half hours unless it's a code red.
Don't know what color the code might be,
but I don't think it's a red.
Three and a half hours drone by
and no ambulance.
We call again.
It'll be three and a half hours unless it's a code red.
Your father is not the only patient the ambulance is for.
I was gonna say fuck you but didn't.
Uncle Bob calls Cousin Jeff.
Jeff calls Saint John's and another ambulance service
is there in forty minutes.
My computer desk chair has wheels on it,
so the ambulance men move him into the living room
that way and get him on their gurney.
Bring my glasses, he says.
He can't see much without his glasses.
The ambulance is not only for him.
I'd run an ambulance up that arrogant asshole's asshole.
The apartment is now mine, alone.
Sunday can take a long time in ending.
Some Sundays do not take the day off.
Some Sundays just don't sing.

Done Deal

In my time of bumping up against formidable people and objects,
I've tried to keep a clear head.
As I shuffle through cities of mad and sad,
I retain my right to bounce off-key.
In the ongoing hours of pain and shame,
when the magic carousel breaks,
I maintain my collapsing harmony.
Yodel your pseudonym in the fugitive rain.
Any name can eventually learn to do.
In the confused rooms of the heart,
no one walks away clean.
The Border Patrol stepped over the line.
Nothing's a done deal any longer.
You empty your past's pockets,
put it all on the big table under the relentless sun.
Nobody cares all that much,
their own agendas drive hard bargains.
I drove a hard bargain insane.
I asked it too many movie trivia questions.
We were waiting for anything to come and get us.
The light in your eyes changes too fast
for me to safely access your crosswalk.
In our days of struggle,
in our nights of unrest,
peace shall open a checking account.
Spend yourself wisely,
eternity doesn't accept credit.
Wait for the water to subside.
Examine the address of your spirit.
The neighborhood is changing.
The landscape mutates.
Democracy is coming back home to America,
the deaf kids sing.
We climb up on our hallelujah pogo sticks.
The quiet chapter will be reading us very soon.
Let your hair down and out.
The exit sign at the end of the long dark hall
still has time to shine on us.

No Dollar Will Do Saloon

Conscience rode in alone
from North Country.
Hard experience free for everyone, take what you can sustain.
Law thaws slow.
Might be needed to perform for the last show.
Heard the fiddler did some time.
Oh, he invented it.
Come and tell your momma about no more language problems.
Come and dance with my parole officer.
They got the large table in the back overloaded with food.
The food it has a history.
The food it done wrote books.
You remember the books.
They spelled our names all day and all night.
They spelled our names when our names did jail time.

Conscience got a room
upstairs at the No Dollar Will Do Saloon.
Let's go up and have a round.
Let's explore our empathetic, done in, gone crazy common ground.
Heard the fiddler knows a few secret rooms.
Oh, he built them.
Come and tell your daddy where the sun just might show up soon.
Come and dance with my daughter's parole officer.
They got the large heart in the back overloaded with love.
The love it has a history.
The love it done wrote books.
You remember the books.
They drew our pictures all day and night.
They drew our pictures when what we looked like did jail time.

Conscience got a movie deal
upstairs at the No Dollar Will Do Saloon.
Cast it well.
It's all in the casting.
I won't cast any first stone.
Come and tell daddy and momma about the pain.
Come and dance your pain.
The love it is our history.
The love it wrote our names.

It Came from Beneath the Anything That Would Have It

In the classic horror epic
It Came from Beneath the Anything That Would Have It,
tense cheerleaders learned that not all forest rangers have botanically
sound skin.
What you take for granted
could bite you in a tender moment.
I saw this film many times.

I didn't know if it was it
or me
in the scene where scientist Axiom Mediocre
discovers the source of humanity's hatred for anything resembling humanity.
I was possessed by an urge to crawl under my seat
and learn the overrated art of Latin.

Some of the extras used in the major panic sequences
once broke bread with buffalo that claimed they were beat.
I saw footage of it on the Poetry Channel,
the one that keeps burning in front of your eyes
when you attempt to decipher it.

It came from within your empty wallet.
It has many long ugly talons.
It claims God sent it.
Don't be too sure.

The other day Glenn Beck interviewed it.
He told us all it would be the ultimate revelation.
However, the thing
calmly sucked Glenn into its huge mouth
and never came clean.

It comes from your deepest paranoia.
It comes from the Mideast and East Texas.
It wants to marry into your family's meltdown.

It came from five corners, the corner drugstore,
it is born in every halfway house and shelter
looking for a manger.
It comes from your hit parade and your wailing wall's plans
to refurbish.

It only demands a good time forever.
It simply asks that you feed it the correct change.
And if you can't hang onto the guardrail
it'll be anybody's game.

It rode with Villa, walked on water with the Jesus boy,
it slept with Alexander the sometimes somewhat great,
it rubbed Romulus and Remus in the hootchie-koo section.

It breathes fire when Stupak dissembles.
It wants you to turn your other ass cheek
when it comes time for its next frenzy.

I asked it in once.
I was that lonely.
It looked at the book I was reading
and ran away making a very irritable sound.

It comes from not hearing what you claim you listened to already.
It comes from supposedly staring down the universe, and
yet you've never even come close to glimpsing a thing.

When it sings
your ears will melt.
When it asks you your name
you'll stammer
all day and all night.

Don't unduly worry,
the night crew is putting out a few sandwiches and cookies.
Tell them what movie wants you to star in it today.
It will come again for you soon.
It will tell you how much it loves you.

Believe it or not,
none of it really requires too much stamina on your part.
Phone it in.
Let the missiles fly where they will.

It may be a horror.
It may be the beginning of the end.
Or maybe
the cockroaches will begin to dress in tuxedos
and the fading wallpaper of our hearts
will once more
feebly shine.

The Ballad of Sam and Galen (An Outlaw Folk Song)

The Landsberg Boys just robbed the last train of thought.
No lawman can reach their apogee.
The coyotes howl their praises
as the mesa begins to hum.
Sam and Galen did it for us folks,
claims a fugitive rainbow on its way to precarious immortality.
Mountain Man Kalbrosky,
in a lucid rare interview with the myopic newsman from town,
said,
Sam and Galen
are on a first-name basis with
Hootenanny,
and no encroaching civilization
can come close.
What shall civilization think? mumbled the news guy.
Sam and Galen invented civilization,
spat Mountain Man Kalbrosky,
who then shift-shaped into an eagle
and flew off for a much-needed vacation
in the border town of Boogaloo,
population 3½,
don't ask me about the ½,
can't begin to tell if the glass
is half a glass.
Sam and Galen once rode with the Barry Smolin Gang.
Oh, you recall those days:
martial law,
Marshal Dillon,
martial arts.
Barry Smolin's name struck nerves
and whenever he told someone to light a Sabbath candle
they dang well did,
even if there weren't any candles around.
Such was the West
in that time and place,
when every red-blooded American boy
was an Apache,
playing saxophone

as the sun
wrote its memoir,
but readers complained,
it's too hot to handle.

One Day Summer Rented a Room

Hard laughter in a can, a bright can, aisle 56,
endurable can, endurable bright hard laughing can.
Can I, would I, should we, hard hard hard laughter in the land,
cool front moving in on,
cool front moving,
sad coffee hallelujah.

Man stumbles up alongside me.
Man says can I sing him some everlasting everloving?
Says me, yeah I can, and commence to let it all fly.

Cool cool front hanging in the back,
easy sorrow in a can, a bright can, aisle 58,
endurable can, endurable bright easy sorrow can.
One day summer rented a room.
I fit into it.

Woman stumbles up alongside me.
Woman says can I dance her some altogether alltime?
Yes says me, yeah I can, and still commence to let it all fly.
Don't matter how brokedown or busted, how forgot or lost,
the flight ability starts here.
One day summer rented all its rooms.
We all fit in.

Texas Hold Em
for Dave Alvin and Peter Case

The fish bite eerily fierce sometimes.
Just hope they don't bite you.
The water tastes like creosote.
Must've been something the sky said.
It'll take a working heart to adjust this volume,
it'll take a poet who can sing
the name of the angry gods' current game of choice,
Texas Hold Em.

What if you've never been to Texas,
can you still hope to hold them?
All sorts of incriminating things try to yank it out of your hand.
Just what in the hell is the it you're supposed to hold onto?
The life preserver, the golden notebook, the rosary that
sings like Rosie Flores?

It'll take a true storyteller to clarify this insanity.
Two good boys came to my soul this morning.
The world was on fire, the world was in pain.
These gentlemen began to sing
and the angry seas parted,
revealing a whole lot of empathetic wounded troupers dancing
across the consciousness of the land.

Dave and Peter see me through.
Their music is my national résumé,
their tunes wave forever on my flagpole.
When the rockslide gets too close,
I open my spirit's hearing aid and let their songs ride in.
Dave and Peter went up the mountain,
reckon it doesn't matter which one,
take your pick.

They rambled up Mount Merle Haggard,
they sailed the Woody Guthrie Ocean.
David Olney and John Prine were aboard the raft as well.

Dave held the helm,
Peter caroused the compass.
The angry gods took a few steps back,
their intensity deflated.

Zeus and Hera own all the Alvin-Case oeuvre.
Pan even plays flute to them.
The old neighborhood just met its new population.
Big Joe Turner smiles down upon everyone.
The name of the game is hang on, no matter what state you're in.
Dave and Peter begin to sing.
Attila the Hun joins the Peace Corps.

Contrary Feelings, California

Contrary Feelings, California, where the skin
doesn't need to keep time and the ushers
walk you, in your sleep, to a large fire at
the edge of the runway where we all gotta
get out our harmonicas and let the good folks
know it takes a rock to do a roll . . .

Contrary Feelings, California, where von Bismarck
fell in love with Thumbelina and the doctors
were all hidden in the rough, waiting for the
Magna Carta to whistle Dixie and let the
overtimers go home and play . . .

Contrary Feelings, California, soft-shoe, two-bit moon,
gumshoe voodoo, lemme swing one with you, they got
apple carts waiting for some reliable horses to
get out of jail, they got avenues waiting for you to
call them by name, lemme paint the ceiling one night
with you . . .

Contrary Feelings, California, the action sees less work than
the actor, folks will come right up to you and offer to finish
your autobiography for you, knowing how tiring it can be,
driving that shift, especially when rush hour finds you
wherever you are trying to kick off your shoes . . .

Contrary Feelings, California, last episode on Sunday night,
all you gotta do is be. Soft-shoe, two-bit moon,
lemme swing one with you.
Them avenues be waiting
for you to call them.
Lemme paint anything
with you.

Truckdriving Momma Don't Hesitate Blues, the Director's Cut

There's a rattler, coiled, ready to strike, sleeping in the gold cup.
The jukebox eats your coins, promises to behave, then plays every selection
you hate.
Best get Truckdriving Momma
on the case.
She walks and talks mountains and fresh air.

There's a major controversy
involving minors
standing on ledges
made of confetti.
Everyone packs a gun.
Everyone claims they enjoy heat.

I saw a charming monkey
give a press conference.
The monkey scratched its ass.
The reporters all applauded.
Bring me my hurricane.
Bring me my front lines.

Truckdriving Momma used to lift some mean weight,
but then serenity rubbed her neck.
She plays cards with the village elders,
who never are too sure
if they're real.
Get some close-ups in the pitch black.
We need to clarify plot threads.

Truckdriving Momma once slung it in Bombay.
Put me on my back.
Give me a little traction.
The monkey picked everyone's nose.
The editors rolled around.

Truckdriving Momma School of Broadcasting
will turn your larynx blue.
Some dogs piss for free.

I saw a strange experience on hind legs.
It was about to fall down and die.
I gave it no quarter.
I gave it a dollar bill.

Truckdriving Momma
she said watch your p's and q's.
I look left.
I stumble right.
Everyone looks so unfamiliarly the same.

Truckdriving Momma she done gone opera,
arias hang from every tree.
Little people
they carry a big load.
Some dogs are just too quiet
when the sky lifts its leg.

Hacienda of Lost Souls

We begin your journey
by telling the Dixie cups
what you did for a living.

One monument
sued another.
The lawyers spoke super fast
and got everyone's order all mixed up.

The Hacienda of Lost Souls
is taking its siesta
to a new daring plateau.
Plateau experts argue
about which socks should go on what feet.

Tuesday stole Wednesday's hair color.
You gotta be careful about who you talk to
when the airliner you're on
decides to try and drown.

Donald Duck was caught waterboarding one of his obstreperous nephews.
A posse got named.
Flamenco dancers work graveyard
at a factory afraid of the dark.

How long have you had your finger in the dike?
Do you really think all that liquid about to flood you out
is water?

Buddha got a dog.
Told the dog to rub Buddha's belly.
In return he taught the dog's collar
to smile.

It's a hard road, sometimes,
the philosopher said, giving me a wink with his nudge.
The tollbooth got a hernia.

Lazarus said, don't wake me too early.
This morning the whistle still decided it had one blow left in it.
The master of ceremonies got lockjaw.

The concierge gave me a secret recipe.
It's so secret
that if I tell it to you
they'll disappear me.

The long and the short
they arrived, yet to be seen and heard from and of.
They sit in the food court,
waiting for all things frozen to one day hopefully
thaw.

Something, I Guess

Something, I guess, bit little Omar Fool.
Bit him in the dark end of the school.
He needed being bit, the arresting cops say,
ever since Omar turned down his Huntz Hall negligee.
Gotta all be a victim or run for president.
Some meandering neurotic is the prevailing resident.
Hit songs just peter out when the dark holes implode.
The number one movie is *When the Dead Men Rode*.
Omar, Omar, the cheerleaders bleed,
one of these days an angry god will teach you to read.
Something, I suppose, ate little Omar Fool.
Being ate is okay if you follow the rule.
Something, I guess, drives nearly everyone insane,
men so tall they blot out the sun.
Coffee's on.
Relax, suck a bullet.
Gotta run.

Missing in Action Just Got Home Blues

God, run quick and get your gun,
there's a temptress in baby Jesus' undies.
Shucks, God said, falling on his head,
let the boy rock.
One day on the big Mississippi,
Jim and Huck asked my name.
I told them about Uncle Wiggly.
He disappeared in Connecticut.
What a crying shame, the apple tree agreed.
Ayn Rand used to live here and bleed.
Missing in Action Just Got Home Blues
on the tongues of all,
I'm Still Looking for Our Room Number
was the best song of any year.
God, run quick and fix my color TV.
Yes, baby.
In the down time,
I can pull your oxen,
I can talk you blue.
Tarzan once
quietly,
in passing,
said
that Jane,
she know how to make a man
swing.

Two Killers Having a Mediocre Coffee Break

I killed him all day long.
I killed him forever.
He keeps getting up.
He doesn't understand the rules.
I kill you, you stay dead.

Yeah, I hear you.
A lot of ornery victims these days.
No tradition, respect.

I don't like my bullets anymore.
I must be getting old.

Yeah, I come home after a long day,
I creak all over.
Maybe it's time for a gold watch.

I dunno, what with the way things are financially.
Plus you got these rabid religious freaks
killing everybody in the room.

Yeah, no style,
no class.

I killed him upstairs.
I killed him downstairs.
I killed him in the middle of his favorite film.

The films today, not much,
frankly.

Momma wanted me to be a vet.
Maybe I ought to hang it up.

I never hung anybody.

I guess you gotta work for the state
to pull that one off.

I never wanted to work the state.
I like freelance.

I killed him where he sang.
I killed him where he loved.
How many times did I kill him?
And he still got up and smiled right through me.

Well, you're the kinda guy,
you could smile through with ease.

Meaning?

Not much. I'm just working my jaw.

Yeah, sure. Got to work the jaw.

If you don't, it'll rust.

Can't have that.

You going to Ed's Christmas party?

Didn't get an invite.

Oh . . . You might still.

I dunno . . . I'm feeling more alone these days.

It happens.

I killed him in his dreams.
I killed him in his myth.

All power to you.

Thanks.

Don't mention it.

And you?

I'm going to a seminar on the use of poison.

Oh, that might be fun. Think you'll meet someone there?

Well, I won't say no, but I can't claim yes.

No, best not to claim anything . . . ever.

Yep, it'll only come back to haunt you.

I killed him in his infancy.
I killed him in his senility.
I killed him on the dance floor.
I killed him in God's outhouse.

God let you into his outhouse?

It was a special occasion.

Oh . . . I'm envious . . . I haven't had a special occasion in years.

Well, you never know.

Gotta run. Be good.

Yeah, sure. Someone has to.

The Angry Stupid People

The angry stupid loud people confess they would like to rule the Earth.
They just need to find out first where it lives.
They've been tossing bones over their shoulders for years.
They are determined to recant the hit parade.

The stupid angry people submerge themselves in kerosene.
They ignite themselves and calmly boast, we are the light!
The stupid angry people smash, gouge, cut, kick, and bite.
They do it for love and God and country.

They continually thread someone else's eye through the big needle.
They claim they walk tall with glory
but then replace their stilts every night.
Time for me to go down my rabbit hole.

All the hat sizes indeed have gone mad.
The queens and kings suffer acute eloquent lockjaw.
The specious carnival barkers who call themselves hard-working legislators
hum broken syntax through gold bullhorns.

The stupid angry people break one another's legs
then swear they'll painfully crawl the extra inch
in the name of what belongs to them.

When they pollute the already sickened air
with their hot wind,
all you can do is get someone to staple your ears closed.

They've been at it for centuries,
ever since the first con man pointed a seemingly viable finger
at the impossible mythical kingdom of Take What's Yours and Fuck the Rest,
and in keeping with the Resonant Book of We Know What's Right,
if you take four seconds too long in giving us our rightful due,
we'll commence to slicing off your fingers and toes.

The angry stupid people drink their own blood
as if it was truly holy.
I drank my blood once,
it didn't make my dancing any more agile.

The stupid angry people wrap themselves in false headlines
and nervous sightseers develop eye strain
if they look too long in their direction.
Time for me to get smoked by something humane.

The wolves waltz around, well-heeled and most defiantly packed.
The mutant depot doesn't know what form the trains it
supposedly loves to sleep with
will now assume.

The angry stupid people all claim God sent them.
Fuck you, I answer,
God sent me instead.

I really didn't want to come to this soirée
but God told me if I came,
he'd introduce me to some very good herbs,
maybe a viable human.

I really didn't argue,
my water's been tasting odd these recent days.
So here I am,
the true stupid son.
I've come to kick your can's asshole.

No more time for stupid anger.
The clock's about to reject your banal sense of time.
The beckoning holes in the firmament are richly getting deeper.
The sand is learning to suck us up quick.

The stupid angry people
stare bewilderingly at themselves in the bathroom mirror.
They just don't know what they see.
Their eyes hurt,
their tiny brains throb from trying to comprehend.

I give them all bricks, knives, guns.
I tell them if you truly believe in love,
you'll know what to do.

Maybe all these angry stupid people
made me an angrier more stupid person.
I admit it,
I'm no better or worse than them.

My tiny heart constricts.
The Seven Wonders of the World
all have seizures
simultaneously.
Call the celestial paramedics,
this is some code blue.

Tell the kid on the corner with the forlorn eyes
to play another guitar lick.
Tell him to sing one last chorus.
Make it believe him when he sings it.

The stupid angry people all praise God.
God kisses them in their fevers.
Guess God got his flu shot.

Tell the kid to close his guitar case,
the monsoon is due any second
and there's only one dinner special left on the shelf.
He'll need something to go by.
He'll need a map you can read.

I'd read him a poem
one day
as soon as the blood dries.

The stupid angry people at times
fall asleep.
May that moment come soon.
I got one hand on the brake.
I got one hand on my soul.

Tell my bed not to fall asleep.
They say it stops hurting bad
after two a.m.
It's 1:59 a.m. and change.

The stupid angry people will sleep in.
Do not awaken them.
In their dreams
they glow,
own the entire universe,
they never die,
they never go old.

Don't tell anyone within striking distance.
I got my stake.
I know where the stupid angry people sleep during the day.
Hold my calls,
I'm going to be a tad bit
busy.

Sink or Swim or So I've Been Told, But I Could Have Heard It Wrong

1.

Don't disappoint the pointed head blocking your view of the
final exciting ten action-filled minutes
of this movie that claims it's based
on your life.
But maybe I went into the wrong screening room,
as there are about 569 screens in this cineplex
and I get confused very very easily
these days,
seemingly.
The young lady who handed me my popcorn
had tattoos in her eyes
and they actually were singing in Gaelic.

2.

Sink or swim or so I've been told
more than once
by folks who never got within 45 feet of anything
masquerading as water.
I could have heard it all wrong.
A civil war was reenacted in my ears and
I'm still in post-cannon smoke rehab.

3.

Litmus failed its test.
It will not get a driver's license this year.
Mr. and Mrs. Litmus are fervidly red.
They need to unwind.
Take some compost over to them and rub it gentle
into their pores.
Standard pores just published their list
of argumentative topsoil.
You'll only be able to trim a few inches.

4.

I'm from the delta, said the ragged guitar,
sitting all by its lonesome
in the fourth and final quarter section
of the room's ongoing belligerent proposition.
I've got a deltoid, someone chimed in
and began to make that ragged guitar
tell us all where we went wrong.
Well, maybe we went right,
because if you go too right,
you wind up falling into a black hole
and sometimes you just love how mysterious
the inside of a black hole might seem.
But then your head hits the curb
and all your voodoo runs out of moxie.
The guy with the deltoid
told government lack of officials that
his name was Del Mercy
from Sometime Soon, Arkansas.
The guitar from the delta
answered to the handle
Flame Central.
Sure, I'll buy it,
with what loose change I have left.
If you're gonna be a flame that intends to burn,
best to be a central flame.

5.

In the super grudge rematch to end all grudge rematches,
Godzilla kicks Tokyo's ass
once more.
But Tokyo knows how this is done.
They claim they are wards of the court.
The court has too many wards,
but who really knows?
Godzilla, satiated for now,
realizes tourism can be good for huge lizard types.

He tells Tokyo that he'll bring in some contractors
to rebuild all the burned-down-and-out
neighborhoods he's created.
Destruction, quips Godzilla,
is the beginning of restoration and construction.

6.

Last night a huge leg came through my telephone receiver.
It said, need a hand?
I said, if I did,
could you become one?
I'm amiable, said the huge leg.
I'm Scott, said me.
At least I used to be.
Not too sure anymore.
I could have got that wrong, too.
Maybe I really was Spot all these years
and misheard Scott.

7.

Come here, Spot, somebody said.
I wagged my brain
and off I went.

The Dancer Steps Forward

The dancer stays home
digging in his earth,
looking for the bone that will
sing to him.

His friends have run off to Europe.
They groan, pull their hair, wail,
America is a paltry place for the imagination.
They hit the walls, deny their past.
They become good Europeans.

The dancer shrugs in his New Jersey afternoon,
begins to dance
around the circumference of his native ground.
I've got to learn the language, he says.
I've got to follow through on the syntax.
There is a music here. Don't be so quick to deny it.

He steps out onto the American earth.
People come to him, ask,
do you know what they are doing across the sea?
They are writing epics!
They are tearing up the linear fabric.

Let me do my digging, he says,
and the music that is alive there
begins to attach itself to his skin
in that hard-working New Jersey afternoon.
His patients come, his patients go.
The good doctor knows there is a music
here.

One of his good friends,
an old schoolboy pal
who will later do time for mixing aesthetics and politics,
keeps haranguing him to come to Europe.

I'm too busy digging, he says,
there is a music here, I tell you,
and my job is to find it,
learn it,
sing it.

You can have your poets of Provence,
you can have Confucius.
I'm hunting a different game altogether.
The sun grows hot.
He begins to sweat there in the yard,
digging.

He takes a drink of water.
We leave him at his work
as night quietly shows up.
Later he steps onto the front porch.
He will begin naming the new rhythm,
the kind of rhythm that you recognize
on the street, maybe.

Not some secret arcane language,
not some language you need a dictionary to understand,
the kind of rhythm
you can maybe
figure out all by yourself
as you roll it around in your mouth,
as you begin to say it and it begins to sing you.

There is a music in the American idiom,
he says,
and wipes his face for the last time,
and begins to think about going up to bed.
Tomorrow is another song.
Tomorrow will be other patients and
words to discover and stories behind such words
that illuminate.

The game, after all
is one of discovery.
The day you stop finding out things
is the day
you might as well
turn yourself in for good.

He slowly makes his way upstairs to
his beloved Flossie.
There is a music here.
All you have to do is believe,
and the rest
is just
some history of
song
and love.

Elastic Town

In Elastic Town
all of us are stretched too thin.
Be gentle when you toss your rocks at us.
Remember that bruises too are countries.

In Maybe So Town
everyone has a story about to tell them.
Some of them need to take time to breathe.
The air can get a bit giddy.
Remember that choking still isn't a crime.

In Anything Can Do Town
we sleep once in awhile.
The beds that claim us,
they've been drinking.
They move across the floor
when you attempt to lie down comfortable.
The longtime silent mountains
started out as talkative piles of dust.
We go wherever the dance instructor asks us.
We wedge ourselves through tiny cracks.

In Elastic City
you disappear for years
then bring yourself back home.
We stumble together
onto the porch,
front or back,
who can tell.
You blink and look into me.
I nod in agreement.

In Elastic City
sometimes you do win.
Come along with your badass self.
Nobody ever keeps score.
The cooking fire has our dinner waiting.
All the years that drive a person to their front door.

Put any key you think you've got in the lock
in Elastic City.

In Elastic Town
magic's run away and joined the circus.
Your eyes are rivers.
Your heart is a cafe.
All your friends drink black coffee
for miles around.
Put your tired bones up on the table.
It'll hold.
I just taped the north wind.
It truly,
when you come by,
lets it all rip.
Your soul I saw in the parking lot
of the big good meal in the sky.
In Elastic Town
our bones sing harmony.

Sway Sway Sway

The big gun just went off.
Everybody fell over dead.
The judges give it 100,
but I know they can't actually count past 10.
I went out in search of no miracle.
I had no secret plan.
I figured I'd just keep walking
until the earth fell asleep.
I heard your voice
beneath the ashes and rubble.
I knew you still had it in you.
I knew how to say your name.

Sway sway sway
just a second more.

Sitting Bull told me about his vision
of a guy with long yellow hair falling upside down
from the sky.
I said, then you must be a jazz artist.
The ghosts are complaining that it's too cold.
I'll knit them gaudy sweaters
made up of patterns of no sense.
Sean asks me to waterboard him,
but then he disappears.
Frank Lloyd Wright designs igloos
on the brand-new supersaver highway.
I saw God, the burning prophet
just through town to see an old flame,
said
he's Charlie Mingus,
he'll set
you right.

Sway sway sway
please try and
believe.
Sway sway sway
any way you can.

Toke one for the guardian angel.
Toke one for me.
We're all impressively crazy
in our own particular way.
Just about now
your bones might want to take a break.
Hang onto your working heart.
The time of language might run out of things to say,
but your body speaks rhythms
that teach the earth.

Sway sway sway
and rest will be along soon.

They got the traffic lights working,
and someone just wrote your favorite score.
The lamp in the window that you testify to in the morning,
it might have broken a bit here and there.
I turn it on anyway.
What you see
is more than you'll need to get.
Doesn't matter.

Sway sway sway
through all the bullshit.

They got the sound sort of working
and the long-distance phone call from the heavens
is just a barefoot poem.

Thar She Done Got Blown

In the epic novel Herman Melville by Moby Dick, Esquire,
a big sperm whale is deformed by
a guy named Ahab,
who used to work retail with me
when I was crawling up.
I've now reached apogee
and the gargoyles have asked me to let them in for free.
The broken men and women who walk my spine
are seeking an easier sequel
to their bones.
I live in a pit that gets big when you're good
and shrinks into oblivion
when you fib.
Thar she done
got blown,
Captain Moby bellowed.

The left-wing book club
is making a decent recent comeback.
We meet on the head of a pin.
We read each other
our bill of rights.
The universe used to sing in key.
It could lose some weight.
Maybe it's too thin.
The weather can't make up its mind.
Mind your manners when you ask God for mercy.
Sometimes he's got lots of wax in his ears.
You might have to take off some of your clothes.
Thar she done blew it.

All the king's hearses,
all the queen's sins,
they become children
looking for my head.
I only got one,
but it's just another way of life.

In the beginning,
through the end,
Wild Bill held a dead man's hand.
Rock 'n' Roll knows where you thrive.
Thar she done went under,
and the joke in it all
was all she damn well wanted to do
was
somehow
survive.

In the early morning,
when the knives sharpen themselves,
reach for me through the wire.
Tell me how it goes.
Thar baby,
beyond all known scope,
thar baby,
is where you and I
most assuredly
blow.

Somebody Had To

Lucrezia Borgia and Lizzie Borden were drinking my tea
when a giant gila monster stuck its tongue out
looking for an easier way.
Somebody had to.

That famous action star
fell into a large hole
in the forehead of the earth.
His manager,
beside himself,
said all surfers will tread water.
Mickey and Minnie Mouse
are slugging it out in my brand-new store-bought eyes.
Go Mickey, I hear a vagrant sing.
Down in the bottom of the bottomless pit
the Three Musketeers fence shadows.
Somebody had to.

Just got back in town.
We're doing breakfast.
When things aren't loud,
it begins with a mandolin
that talks behind your back in Gaelic,
and the moon is nonrefundable.
I hear the seizures.
I've heard the cries.
Swing your lover.
Hold onto trust.
In the dark dark back lots
you don't really
absorb too much.
The holy writ just flunked its orals.
Come inside anyhow.
We got some food.
We got some things to clarify.
Somebody needed to.

Just wrote its name on all
those golden bathroom walls.

Declare who you think you be.
We shoot out of the cannon at ten.
I think my head is a hard planet.
Shake me down, shake me up.
I got a marriage certificate,
the sponge said to the Death Star.
We all go upright
in a room that declares please duck.
Music will get you.
You hopped the final line.
We all have to.

I see you in the replay.
You reach for the magic.
I see you revolving
across what's left of my
mind.
I think it's kick the shoes off for good time.
Just remind the glass on the ground
what the name of your foot is.
The arsenal melts.
The tongue becomes epiphany.
The losing hand
calmly lands.
I see you in the myth,
those stories got you moving.
I hear you in the crazy house.
Everyone is a diva.
Somebody had to.

A reclusive guardian angel
attempted to
sing.
His foot was a city.
His heart slept in the park.
What the name of your foot is.
Every leg will find a shoe.
Calmly, we land.
The myth tells you its name.
Attempt to
sing.

The Raymond Carver Two-Step

It's when you think you've run
out of dance floors
and those hard-to-understand
walls
just demand
so much of your skin.

When all the languages gnawing on your lobe
seem to go on and on
with nothing much to ask you,
let alone teach you.

It's when the cold
steps into your underwear,
the night turns its back
on your heart.

It's times like these
you need to feel someone
can ask you out into the unknown territory.
Someone to intersect his or her blood
with your own.

There in the howling center of all things,
there in the cries of all things dreaming,
the fires I hear speak a common river.
Broken bones hibernate in cool oxygen
learning new rhythms
of skin.

Raymond Carver
felt
the music in the silence of the music.
He wore his river strong.

When the IOUs pile up past your throat,
the firing squad spells your name correctly on their bullets.

When the airplanes seem to want to crash on your head
and your head
only,
times like these.

Raymond Carver's feet lived in real earth.
His fingers danced on the skin of stars.
His people wanted their shot at song,
even if their mouths were numb.

He gave them a dance floor,
even when they felt they had run out.
He gave them longitude and faces.
He gave them latitude and skin.
He simply
gave.

**The Admitting Room in Your Heart Just Might
One Day Get Overfilled**

A deep hole woke up this morning,
right where epiphany's shoe sizes were rumored
to have taken up residence.

The talk a good fight people have come, gone.
They overstayed the oxygen with their welcome.
Some of them beat the snare drum of their skin with verve.
The majority, though, broke down
when a wounded gnat crawled through.

The boat that told the world it would successfully float us home
just discovered the mutual respect of leaks.
You didn't really expect to get a ticket out, did you?
The admitting room of the heart
just might be slightly overfilled,
now that all the resonant mattresses
sag whenever you tell them a story.

There was a doctor once.
He had his finger in the hole in the dam.
He sang to his finger.
His finger couldn't understand the words he used.

On the ride back
from the copacetic lynching,
everyone began to attract flies
no matter what college they attended.

Tell the rag and bone man
I'll be along shortly to pay my dues.
Bereavement just announced its intending marriage
to any cognizant pilgrim.

The cold crawled into bed next to us.
It told us it heard noises, was scared.
One of us will have to get our time card punched,
take it for a walk.

The men and women who easily forget what planet they reside on
sweep up the debris.
They look healthy, radiant.
Don't tell me it's as the crow flies.
The crow, you know, fears airplanes,
ever since the disaster of . . .
it'll only hitchhike.

There's a long time coming.
There's a long drop at the bottom of the ladder.
Are you sound?
Can you do one-handed push-ups like Jack Palance?
Did you see the state of the world this morning?
Utter disarray.
Tell the art department to send someone capable.
There's a hole in the forehead's foreclosure.
It widens every time someone dies.
Soon it will be so magnificent in its vastness,
anybody will be eligible to topple in
and become a statistic.

Please pull the burning dobro out of the fire.
It might not work so well these days
but it knows where I live.

Across the room that never stops unfolding,
love takes its hourly beating.
Tell makeup we need something to wash the blood.
When you tire of playing warrior
maybe you can relearn how to simply live.

The Day the German Kid Came into Dutton's
Looking for *My Sweet Charlie*

Sometimes,
not often,
you can smile at how
things turn out.
For 23 years,
I worked the fiction room at Dutton's Books
in Brentwood, West Los Angeles,
the former home of Marilyn Monroe, Mickey Cohen,
and that O.J. guy.
I stood behind a counter,
talking books,
selling a few.
I wasn't above putting my own stuff
on the counter.
Is this you? they'd ask.
Yes, and I'll sign it for you if you buy it.
They did, usually.
When Dutton's bought Brentwood Books,
October 1984,
I'd been there four years,
all in one room.
By the time the whole show
went under,
we'd gone to three rooms around an open courtyard,
and a coffee shop.
I have many memories of those days.
I never took my work home with me.
Once I was out the door
I was a free man.
One of my favorite days
was when a young German kid
came in looking for David Westheimer's great novel
My Sweet Charlie,
which TV turned into a film
with Patty Duke and Al Freeman Jr.

I said,
sorry,
it's out of print.
He needed it for school.
I'd always curse those teachers
who assigned books out of print
to their students.
However, I knew Westheimer
lived in the neighborhood.
He was a nice guy.
I said to the kid,
hang on,
maybe I can do something.
I called the Westheimer home.
David was in.
Hey, I said, I got a kid here who wants *My Sweet Charlie*,
what do you think?
Ten minutes or so go by.
David comes in smiling,
shakes the kid's hand,
has a copy of the book for him.
The German kid's jaw drops.
They go out and talk a bit.
I feel good.
I like to feel good.
You can't always feel good.
I hope that kid scored an A on whatever he had to do
regarding that read.
I don't recall what the weather was like
that day.
Do you?

Doughnut Kill

Bad open mic poetry night.
God shows up with a long, long, long poem.
Something about the Doughnut Kill,
how the soft shoe still exists.
Governments stumble in, hair in eyes.
They all want at least five minutes.
Someone once produced this stuff, I guess,
or so the rumor goes.
Now it's catch as catch can.
Catch can sure do a lot these days.
Did you see Catch last night on TV?
God finally finishes the long, long, long, poem
about the Doughnut Kill.
There is quiet in the house.
Quiet has its own room at the end of the upstairs hall.
Quiet has a suitcase full of enlivening photos.
The Doughnut Kill, I remember that,
the crossing guard at the corner says.
I trust the crossing guard at the corner,
something in his skin, I guess.
Bad open mic poetry night is almost over.
Doughnut Kill with Robert Mitchum and Lee Marvin,
the musical,
of course.

When Santa Had Claws

Santa spoke in tongues.
I stammered, I've been good.
Maybe I lied.
My two brothers played trombone.
I played my tongue.
Glib rowdy asshole,
I was easily identified as
by Santa's elves,
who worked for a right-wing cabal
that you could only
decipher on cable.
Santa had a Luger
he got on a layaway plan.
I can take over the North Pole,
maybe even the world.
This was in the day
Santa had claws,
but no escape.
His sled was bulletproof.
His reindeer were rakes.

The Devil Had Nothing to Do With It . . . I Did It All By Myself

Quit telling me the Devil made you do it.
I saw you use both of your hands.
The last time I saw the Devil,
he was in a rest home,
drooling and being force-fed.
I know what you're truly capable of.
I've seen your X-rays.
The time will be coming over soon.
You'll have to take the fall.
I like to see credit given
when credit is clearly due.
I hate it when you get all modest on me like this.

Maybe God made you do it.
Maybe he whispered in one of your ears.
You always loved it when I whispered.
Call me Iago, Mr. Othello.
Let me walk at your side.
We'll leave scars
in the thighs of the country.
I know you can handle all the publicity.
The coffee gets grounded kind of loud.
The diapers of the rising famous
are covered in blood.

Come on, big boy,
let me see you make a fist.
So much seemingly indestructible meat.
So very little strength.
The clouds are full of ambushes.
The doorman won't recognize you.
The Devil owns a brokedown motel
on a highway that has no friends.
Lemme help you make the bed.
Then you gotta lie in it.
Take your time.
The phones work only when they want.

The Devil ate something mean.
He's been in the office toilet for hours.
When he finally wanders out
give him some ice cream.
The dinosaurs retired:
too much negative press.
Feel the wind?
It's gonna want to get your name.

God, He Forgets His Bags

He calls customer service.
The big yellow suitcase,
my kingdom sleeps in it.
One morning,
when the barnyard cried foul,
all the roosted chickens
came home too.

The Devil likes God's tattoos.
I was in a passing fancy phase, God says,
looking at all the waitresses and waiters
that are constantly asked by hungry diners
about the weekly special,
love.
The dishwasher saves us.
The monsters are brought back down to earth.

God and the Devil fuck.
They do it so sweet.
Call the 800 number.
Get me some much-needed relief.
When the big house broke up,
when the labor laws died from toting too much,
the navy just sank.
The doorbell rang.

God and the Devil joined at the hip,
Siamese bimbos the both of them.
They best stay put
and not venture into my end of town.
I see you fragile.
I'll back you up all the way in your lawsuit to not become dead.
I hear you crying
in the family hour time.
I'm cutting through the sheetrock.
I'm mumbling up my acceptance speech.

The Devil was way too busy learning to behave.
I did all of this
by myself.
The horses are snorting in disgust.
The cosmic game plan is blowing all over the floor.
Come on baby,
the hay is piled high.
Let's take a roll.

The Devil and God
just had their third baby
today.
I lift my hand to keep the sun from slurping my brain.
Come on baby,
don't you finally
feel
it's time for
you to come in
out
of the
rain?

Roll those Dice, Blind Man, Let the Whole Damn Thing Rip . . .

Come on with your bad self.
Make the roof beams capitulate.
Raise your uncle's ante.
Climb the shrinking mountain.
The boys and girls you once were
grew up to become jail cells.

I wanted to discover a cure for humanity.
I stubbed my toes on Ponce de Leon's Fountain of Vermouth.
The big parade just got knocked over by a motorcade.
The high-powered rifles all sing in tune.
Come on and explain your lack of a reflection in the mirror.
Make the dying finally get dead.

The master of ceremonies
is the best servant going.
They asked Sisyphus to be a guest Rock critic.
I don't think he digs my sound.
In the bowels of the U-boats of tenderness,
in the dayroom they have cake.

Shock treatments ask you for a small stipend.
Got to keep the planet from deflating.
The right honorable Billy Saul Nowhere,
I'll keep his talons off your baby
long enough to lead us to salvation.
As you know,
Sal Vation is a great crooner.
He makes the Majorettes sweat.
Roll those dice, blind man,
let the whole damn thing rip.

I've been trying to find the last piece of the puzzle
for way too long.
My back isn't amiable.
My head forgot how to enunciate.
Raise your hand if you remember the best time you thought you had.
In the giant trash heap,
once in awhile you find traces of gold.

Rock me baby rock me across the brokedown palace's grandchildren.
Tell the scavengers the cupboard is bare.
A new suit of armor is on its way.
The cantankerous goodwill jester
gestured a slight bit obscene
when his waitress began to wail
one of those all-night affairs,
with real scary emotions that no law could tame.

Catch me as I split in three.
One of me wants to crawl under the futon.
One of me blots out the sun.
One of me siphons epiphany
from any passing belief.

Take my best profile out to dinner.
The food might declare war any minute.
Reckon it'll remedy its dislocation.
The red carpet is illiterate.
The purveyors of knowledge, purloined,
catch my next number
as it falls from the lips
of mimes.

In the glorious age,
at the bottom of the shit hole,
the bright affable vermin
were making lots of noise about how resonant
they were.

Once upon a time,
when the clocks all said don't tell me a thing,
once upon a drowning attempt of a sea,
the fault lines in our better natures
grew affable tone poems
filled with ambidextrous sightseers
naming the new road.

Roll those uncontested drunks.
Let the choir break their voices
trying to catch up.
The market's value wavers.

In the gut-wrenching heat
a cool glass of Maybe I Can
suffices.

Between changes of guard
the planners, shapers, movers, and bosses
all get catatonic
when you begin to shimmy.
Come on down:
you're the lucky one,
proud owner of a large hole in the fugitive sky,
the embraces we yearn for,
the clothes our hearts wear.

There's a storm moving in,
about five minutes left.
Tell me that joke again
about the god who takes his dog into a bar.
Or was it the dog
who took his god
into that same bar?
It probably was fiercely hot.

The dog, the god,
they came for Happy Hour.
Happy Hour complains too much these days.
It snarls at us when we run past.
We'd snarl back
except all the good snarls
got spoken for,
leaving the rest of us
with postage stamps that keep going up
before we can find a proper envelope
to marry them to.

Let me have those dice, blind man.
It's time for you to cook the big meal.
The whole thing is too ripped to do any more ripping today.
Come back later,
when the molecules are filled with zest
and every mouthful of dirt
tastes like
champagne.

this house claims nobody's home

This House Claims Nobody's Home

The festering wounds all wish to retire early.
Experience demands it sacrifice too much.
Your husband may very well be dead within the week, ma'am,
but this facility requires six thousand dollars up front
in cash before we can
accommodate him.
Best to sell anything you might own,
become a Medicaid recipient.

All our hearts become emergency rooms,
barely audible,
beneath the ever-increasing screams
that pour rhythmically down
from the heights of we need your money, sweetheart,
before we can suture your ever-enlargening
hole.

This house claims you're home.
I set sail through the opaqueness of your eyes.
Batten down the final straw's hatch.

You claim the storm is coming,
but it's been comfortably parked next to me
for days.

Raise your hand
if you remember the ancient days
of the heart:
how it once held court,
how it once led our chorus.

There Is

There is this tiny city at war with itself in my heart.
Its citizens want to dream but have headaches.
They wash themselves in water that just gets you dirtier.

There is this jury wandering the courthouse lawn of my soul.
They don't know what case they're weighing in on.
I'd like to take them to a good movie
but the one theater in town suffered a stroke.

There's a sleepwalking insomniac in my throat.
He'd so much like to perform one last number
before the net comes down.

There is surgery,
remittance, ongoing rain, and empathy.

There is fear, smiles, hate, and I told you so.
They all want a piece of my action
but my action took a late Greyhound out of here hours ago.
The bathrooms on Greyhounds do not like the way I dance.
They lock me in them and ask me to repudiate anything passing through.
I become a tiny country
looking for a pair of socks that match.
Step on me gentle,
I bleed easy.

There is a mandolin coming over to claim me.
I am ready to be named.

There is nothing left to lose.
We've given it all we ever had.
Come now and be easy.
The fractures we are knit themselves whole.

There is a quiet corner not yet assimilated by insanity
that will kiss our scars.
We order breakfast
as the sun of our lives
rises one more time.

Would-Be Greek Tragedy Seeks Chorus
That Can Hold a Tune

All night long the telephone says,
all your wrongs will run for president.
Soothsaying momma with a PhD
holds her own in the dark end of the infirmary.
All day, maybe, the sun will swing.
Graveyard shift is a quirky stream.
Down on the corner I heard a rhythm cry.
Your house is something I could learn to find.

All night long the owl seeks to dream.
Baby, the forest done moved.
Climb a tree, save the Earth, smoke it well.
Soothsaying momma with a PhD
claims she can hustle, used to sing kind of loud.
Baby, who moved the forest on me?
I wanted to be kind of natural
beneath the pleas.

Would-Be Greek Tragedy Seeks Chorus That Can Hold a Tune.
Down on the corner rhythm found me.
Got to believe in something, maybe get seen.
Soothsaying momma stole my PhD,
told me to come back later when the food was hot.
Hold your own in the ongoing infirmary.
Wounds come in all sizes.
Wounds claim they can dream.
Climb a tree, swing with me.
Get a little closer
with your ways and means.

Man Caught Impersonating a Child

Toxic Annie, she just turned 102.
Her face built this city.
She took us dancing
when the clouds phoned in sick.
Come on, tell me where you hide when the shadows get too real.
Deciduous Trudy she just saved her heart
from a very mean-looking jail.
She comes slithering across the grove.
She paints her eyes with vacation time.
She sings the corporeal sound.

Man caught impersonating a child
on a street where only grown men die,
will you see me when the lunches begin to glow?
Man caught writing bad checks
to accounts payable without ability to hear
—soft, close by, dark—
seeks vulnerable chessman
to ask out on date.
Yes, I remember the fish, how they asked us to bite them.
Please let us know you care.
Please take care of the lawn.
They want to show the house soon before the soldiers return.
She comes speaking speakeasies of sometime we cry.
She paints my eyes with vacation time.

Man caught impersonating a man
on a street where everyone comes up to bat
—soft, close by, dark—
seeks companion that can hop.
History stood there in the corner,
trying to keep its alarm clock happy,
on the street where nobody gets along,
on the street where nobody is ever wrong,
on the street where you can still learn how to love.
The good silver trembles
when life enters the room,
as it all should be.

Rest now, put your aching head down on some country that is soft.
Rest now, and treat me to the way.

On the street where the sun used to know
how to bounce,
come come come with me
and bounce bounce bounce.
I got tired from tossing runes.
Got arrested for trying to figure
the middle names of certain moons.
Come, come
—soft, close by, dark—
younger trains, older rain.
The good silver trembles
when life lovingly touches the room.

Man caught doing not much,
but he does it well.
Leave him then,
in the tender skin of yes.
Leave it all close to the end
in the tender skin of yes yes yes yes.
I picked up more runes,
tossed them your way.
I sang it,
no matter what day.

Fact-Finding Committee Hoedown

The fact-finding committee is sitting on the ex-president's face.
They are trying to pass the IQ test.
Name all Seven Dwarves.
Name all the actors who played the Magnificent Seven.

The census-takers are looking for sense,
both common and not so common.
The wolves are getting closer to Main Street.
They smell blood.

Ex-beauty queens form a union to go to war against aging.
The planet continues to revolve.
Sociopaths still dress well.
Guess they can afford it.

They found Joe the Plumber aboard the *Pequod*.
He was hired to flush out Ahab's paranoia.
I'd like to read Moby Dick's memoir,
but he's still working on it.

The fact-finding committee stick their chests out for the photo op.
There are thousands of new cracks in the sidewalks.
There are dark cloud layers in the sky.
They're handing out subpoenas to cockroaches.

Cockroaches are everywhere.
They've seen everything and done it all.
They'll be great witnesses at the hearing.

It's time for Don Rumsfeld to go waterboarding.
It'll make the cover of *Sports Illustrated*.
The predators are looking for stimulus.
Be careful, don't get too close to the fire.

The electricity went out just as the murderer was to have been identified.
It leaves a funny taste.
All of the ambulances are booked.
They keep moving the hospital just when you think you've made it.

The fact-finding committee snorts your bank account.
They turn green.
I feel green is a bona fide color.
Everyone claims they like trees.

The forest is inches closer to town.
Soon nobody will be able to see anyone else.
We'll all have to rely solely on instinct.
Damn, they need a crosswalk here.
The traffic is way past dangerous.

Put your hand on the bleeding Good Book,
raise your right hand,
raise it to the sky.
I swear to . . .

The poker game goes on for days.
Somebody will walk out a winner.
The graveyards are full of winners, and their graves
seem very similar to those of the losers.

The merry-go-round horses come to life.
We'll need somebody to clean up after them.
The fact-finding committee had LSD put in their morning coffee.
The afternoon session should be fun to watch.

At the very end of the process,
their facts pile up in a corner of a warehouse
on the edge of town.

Transients break into the warehouse and sleep
on these piles of facts.
The facts seep into their skins.

The next morning, these transients,
now infected with facts,
move to new locations.
The facts spread and a lot of folks are unhappy.

The king and queen
are just a pair of village idiots.
Makes you want to join a cause.
Any cause.

The fact-finding committee coughs up blood.
Get a specialist down here.
Oops, all the specialists are 100 miles east.
Best to cut your losses and run.

I swear to . . .
uphold, upend, upchuck, up and down we bounce.

Ahab gives Joe the Plumber the magic doubloon.
He found Moby in Ahab's wooden leg.
Everyone now can call it a day.

Did You Know . . .

The Earth is 2/3 Wild Turkey bourbon.
It keeps drinking me.
Tall men have difficulty reading short stories.
The sun is reading a guidebook on how to be perceived as hot.
Munchkins live in Karl Rove's belly.
The Earth is a myth.
It came over for dinner
but didn't bring any wine.
Pike Bishop's Wild Bunch didn't really die at Agua Verde,
they joined the Supreme Court.
It's 2 a.m. Pacific Coast time,
Friday the 13th.
Jason Voorhees works for Citibank.
His machete does not cotton to the Employee Free Choice Act.
I sometimes believe in the humanity of mankind.
Sometimes I fall down and scrape my soul.
I get up and the bull snorts and would like to gore me
but realizes I used to wait on him at this trendy nightclub
where sand became water
and love was not outlawed.
The cars drive themselves insane.
The secretaries have not come back from lunch.
I think I live here somewhere,
just make room for me in the nondescript corner.
There are wounds in the paychecks.
The well seemingly hasn't hit bottom.
Tell everyone I meant well,
my aim was damn inaccurate
but the targets these days just move way too fucking fast.

911 River

Call 911 and make my chicken nuggets free.
Anybody can get into this party, seemingly.
The shallow people hang out in the deep end of the pool.
All that Bush-Cheney unconstitutional fortitude
now being daily revealed,
John Yoo's head on a platter,
eight years of a Justice Department gone insane.
Quick, get the depressants.
Karl Rove as Santa.
His reindeers work for Blackwater.
Risa Mickenberg, the First Lady of everything,
sings Connecticut's for Fucking.
I think the Bush family hails from somewhere around there.
Don't cut my throat
unless you have a knife with a spotless pedigree.

Call 911 and tell them your chicken nuggets were eaten
by terror.
The big reptiles come out swaggering.
Their eyes are green and mean.
They've been rocking out under some fierce sun.
The Taliban are making a strong comeback.
They're having a poppy-growing telethon
on the Daddy Rush cable network.
If I were president,
Luke Askew would be in charge of energy.
The Mousketeers are dropped behind enemy lines.
A special choo choo will race from Disneyland right into your open mouth.
Once again I put obscure cultural sand traps
in your golf course.
Don't forgive me too hard.

I'm diving into 911 River.
There's gold somewhere in the bottomless pit.
I see my fellow humans leaping into it perpetually.
They must have a reason.
The Age of Reason is an old fellow
on a walker

telling lies to moths
who are so determined to continually fly into the bright lights
and self-incinerate.

I'm washing away all sin in 911 River.
Sin comes in all sizes
and is essentially made in factories.
Here comes our own special lynch mob.
They seem wondrous with dedication.
Hope their rope will learn to love the size of our necks.

Been There and Done That

Big exciting news.
NASA is going to land a man on Earth.
He'll chart everything out,
take samples of all the species he finds.
Someone maybe will finally make sense out of the place,
a chaotic planet full of creatures that make loud weird noises.

Loud weird noises finally form their own union.
Their shop steward lives in my left ear.
Have you heard this one?
Been there and done that.

Standing naked in a snowstorm,
trying to learn my lines.
The big scene is coming up.
You need to stay calm.

Long lines of men and women
applying for some kind of future,
they have all their paperwork ready.
You take a number.
You dress warm if you must.

They claim the best cure for insomnia is sleep.
They sell cans of sleep all along the highway.
Big stores stock it,
mom-and-pop places too.

The professor stands before his very large class,
mostly young good-looking ladies.
He begins to tell them the best way to tell time
is to break your watch.
Time will then stand still.
You'll be able to look it in the eyes
and see what's at home there.

I'm joining a notorious big band.
We'll invade your castle.
Make the damndest music you'll ever know.

The UFOs land on Wall Street.
Take me to your leaders, the aliens mutter.
The bank bosses bow and the aliens probe them for hidden gold.
It makes a full-grown anything cry.
Been somewhere, done anything.

The round peg has sharp words with the square hole.
The 1,000+ jigsaw puzzle is missing a piece.
There's a group of terrorists in the coffee.
Run the movie back to its opening credits,
got to make sure who that actor is.
Been him, done zilch.

Broke bread with Alvin the Chipmunk.
The House of Lies,
a fine chain,
just opened a new branch
in my stomach.
Ate that, lived the result.
Felt that, saw the big light in the timid sky.

That man landed on Earth.
He stepped out of his capsule,
translation book in hand.
I bring you love.
Never been there, could certainly use it.

The wild dogs are also forming a collective.
They'll get all their bones together
and build a new community,
shuffleboard and pool table.

The guest lecturer today apparently knows something.
The horses are running.
They know the end of the movie.
I'm going to sit through all the credits.
I got nowhere to go
and my feelings
are out of season.

Mr. Touch and Go

I saw a beaten Earth
clamoring for some kind of payback.
I said, did you need a shoeshine?
Did the escalator break down again?

Rumors sort of have had it.
They claim they are still within range.
Everyone has a best-selling panacea.
Think I need to pound my head a bit.
I want to see stars.

I heard a sobbing person
inventing a new way of life.
I said, did you need a friend?
Could you come back in?

The taxis aren't all yellow,
which makes it difficult
to predict weather,
whether or not you can hold that position much longer.

I've seen the wide-screen presentations.
I've been asked to diagnose microdots.
I need a magenta pogo stick.
I want to bounce with the stars.

Mr. Touch and Go
he just moved in.
He has a way of inhaling.

The planet once had migraines.
It barely clears the rent.
The normal ones don't keep records.

The army just ran away.
I thought I had your crib sheet,
but I mistook the name of the sky.

Mr. Touch and Go
he can't sing a lick,
but he sure likes to hum.

There's This Museum

There's a brokedown museum
on the corner of Get Up and Don't You Start.
The drinks that live inside it
have been tasted by anyone claiming they were once alive.
In the middle of some incoherent summer,
you write your name on the welcome mat's wall.
Seasons hot-wire deranged automobiles
that carry things too far.

There's an unsung law
hiding in the beard of love.
It can't play guitar
and it swears it'll never measure up.
I took it dancing.
I lied about its age.
Smoke pours out of every tenement's refund check.
Potbellies state they're overdue for success.
A man and a woman break down the front door
searching for a place that will remember their password.

There's this museum inside my head.
It wobbles when you touch it.
It sings when
you ask
if it's
okay
to play
dead.
The gaping hole
says, let me bottom out.

There's this museum on fire,
cast out to sea,
in the cold air of not much hope.
The fiddle asks you to leap through imaginary
hoops.
Count the quiet wounds,
lay them smiling on a corner table.

An exit hole once strolled in God's soul.
It got lost in a tired rain.

There's this museum
teeing off
at 5:15 a.m.
Everyone involved
has been requested
to learn to
behave.

Bootleg Love

The producers just won't wait on you any longer.
You better come crawling out of your trailer, outhouse, castle.
The ingenues they are pumping gas
and waiting on their day.
Bootleg love
is the best love,
the kids claim.
They love it when you fall down for free.
They sing your potential
in bathrooms that shine.
The head guy is groaning:
too much load.
He takes in his money.
It makes him bend over.

Bootleg love
shoots to number one.
Everyone gets a pair of 3D glasses.
Nobody ever dies.
I walk around for years.
My shoes fall asleep at my feet.
I listen for my cue.
I memorized my lines.
I like how you roll.
I see you on the mend.

Bootleg love
will save you from the tax man.
It took that poor fellow
out into the woods.
I don't know of any woods that will fit,
but it took him sailing.
They found their yacht
living in sin with a whale.
I don't do judging.
I leave that to the able-bodied.
I sit on my head
making a better deal.

Bootleg love
needs a job.
It can wait on any known table.
It can hold up its end
of the
damn tiring
song.
Okay.
Shine a light.
Tell me the score.
My next drink is in progress.
This world just gets smaller.

Bootleg love
wrote a hit single.
It got lost in the mail.
You can claim a refund.

Brokedown Hallelujah Hootenanny Hoedown

All the broken people are having their three-day annual convention
this weekend,
under the big top.
The keynote speaker
will be a tiny man crushed by a huge obnoxious boulder.
He claims he'll be able to project without a mic.
I don't feel it.

The broken people grow more in number each passing day.
He better use a mic or his throat will go under.
It's getting so economically unfeasible these days,
even assassins are getting laid off.
I'm gonna go myself.

I'm not all that broken, just yet.
But there's a rumor knocking on all the doors of my neighborhood
that a certain magnetic personality,
recently deep deep down on his luck,
will be given a few seconds to perform under the unrepentant spotlight.
As Sparky my talking dog would sometimes have it,
you got to grab what little might accidentally fall your way.
Maybe Sparky can come too.

Dogs get broken just like anybody else.
Are you brokedown, Mr. Sparky? I ask.
He lifts his scowling mug up from his bowl.
Never disturb me when I'm eating, he grumbles.

The Brokedown Hallelujah Hootenanny Hoedown Orchestra
is on tour wherever you happen to be hiding.
They really can belt a tune out of the ballpark.
Their voices shatter the mirrors of Versailles.
I went outside into the epiphany's fever.
I checked myself into repercussion rehab.
All the staff there know my favorite song.
They demanded I sing it to them.

My brokedown hallelujah
forgot its password and couldn't log into its account.
Sparky knows what I need.
He lifts up his leg as if he really knew yoga.
The ensuing river led me to the long-sought sea.
The ship awaiting my pleasure
actually sank only halfway
before calling it a night
on account of rain.

I got my free tote bag of brokedown hallelujahs.
I skipped across no-man's-land.
I gave no quarter, I took no prisoners.
Sparky huffed and puffed right by my side,
admonishing me to keep believing.
Sparky's a true zealot.
He bites down on that rawhide
we call life.
Sometimes he doesn't come up for air
for days.

Ophelia, Get Thee to a Winery

The biggest mistake we ever saw
just moved in.
Give it all you got.
Sell it what little you own.

There's blood in the ironclad agreement.
There are potholes in Eden.
Ophelia she used to shake it.
Then that Hamlet guy rode in.

Ophelia, get thee to the winery.
The sun is looking for some shade.
Paranoia builds a nest on every branch.
Tell the undercover guy to come clean.

Ophelia she's got a red cell phone.
When I fondle it I'm never afraid.
The king and queen
were shocked at the hip.

Ophelia she likes secretive men.
They date in darkened holes.
I guess it's almost time.
Throw those dice.
Let us hear you pray.

On the avenue,
nothing comes easy.
Ophelia she's got the leg.
The coach is burning.
The mice have come home to roost.

When your room is finally prepared,
when the angels ask you to cover the check,
Ophelia puts her arms around you
and all sobbed tears
turn to
chablis.

Something I Must Have Said, as I Don't Remember How to Think

The beasts don't like my style.
Their number one arbiter of what goes
roughs me up whenever I dare to wander through
their end of things.
I'd run to the Beast Police,
but they seemingly aren't all that pleased
with me, either;
every time I go to make a complaint
they grab me and hang me upside down.
The chief of the Beast Police
is fascinated when the blood rushes down to my head,
or so he continually slobbers.
Something I must have said,
as I don't remember how to think,
ever since the day the city went into a temporary coma
for 45 minutes,
and all the shopping malls got pregnant.
Ever since that strange strange time,
all sales have had very hypnotic ways
of pulling you in
to buy buy buy
when you have no no no
money to spare.

Ever since then the most rudimentary chores
zap me and make me turn on
the Waste Your Paycheck Channel on TV.
The beasts slither anywhere they've got the mind to go.
They run all the lights that actually work
half the time.
The beasts think they're tough shit.
The Beast Police leap into the closet
when the beasts get too close.
Something they might have said,
if they could enunciate.
Something they might have thought,
if they had brains that meant.

It gets frustrating for a good-natured sap such as I.
I need to find an endurable atoll
and ooze in quiet and private,
since both beast and Beast Police
have no seeming use for me.
I once read in an insulting yet intelligent magazine
that you should attempt to be of use
to people and things,
even to people who are no more than things.

If you see me hobbling along life's conveyor belt,
don't get startled if I seem a bit awry.
I never fit anybody's game plan,
and my clock ran out of time hours ago.
Best to not worry about the mundane things.
There are way too many of those wherever you attempt to flow.
The beasts and the Beast Police
can work out their mutual destiny
in their own idiosyncratic way.
They certainly don't need me.

I'm stumbling good-naturedly north,
toward the Dobro Mountain,
where they say you can see your best intentions
in the water,
and the dragons there
have quelled their obsession with breathing fire
for no inexplicable reason.
I'm empathetic with that, I guess.
Best to conserve your ability to breathe fire,
save it for those cold lonesome tunes of nights
when the chill siphons the marrow in your
good-time bone structure.

I'm tiptoeing to the big hoedown
that may only live in my feeble brain.
I'd like for you to feel the music,
but if you can't hear it,
I won't try to make you see it as well.
I'll soon leave the county of beasts and Beast Police.

I'll take my chances in the unknown hopeful free and easy.
I truly couldn't be either one.
I don't have the stamina to be a productive-enough beast,
the species would crumble.
I don't have the demeanor to be a Beast Policeman,
a baton looks shitty in either of my hands.

See you soon, maybe
on the dark side of the fugitive moon.
I hear they got some dance halls living there.
They are currently hiding in deep caves,
but I think it's about time
they show up for work.
Send me a tune if you can.
Let me know when you get out on parole.
Don't wake the beasts when you head out.
Don't get mistook by the Beast Police
for something I know you aren't.
I'll leave a light on for you.
Just connect up to the sway.
I packed up all the borders.
I buried them deep.
It's free range from now on,
and your seat at the table
is assured and
happily awaits.

Save Anyone Who Might Be Who You Are

The walls ask if it's okay to come tumbling down
about this time of the afternoon.
Being a sociable-enough sort of person, you acquiesce.
The end is here! Chapter One declaims
from its limo,
carousing through the garbage.
Makes a full-grown anything
want to hide in any closet that will accept it.
Save anyone who might be who you are,
as saving is better than spending, they say.

The maimed would like you to consider helping
them seek refutable mending.
That is, if you've got the time.
I know you are busy these days,
with all this talk of decay and angry people
eating each other,
and it's not even lunchtime.
Maybe you can send one of your minions down
with some Elmer's Glue-All.
Knit those fractures something resonant.

Thank you so much for seemingly caring,
the hangman said to his rope,
I knew I could count on something in this life.
My heart ran out of gas on the side of some tiny road.
I heard there was a place ahead worth going to.
I stood my ground and warbled.
The sun said, call me Sol!
I said okay, Mr. Bass,
thank you for sharing.
Even if the box is empty,
the gesture will suffice.
The avenging army ran out of people to kill.

Now they got to start in
on themselves.
The main feature begins in three minutes.

Too many trailers.
You'll have time for a fast bathroom call.
My head can't see clear any more.
There are way too many burning cities in it
and all that heat makes me dizzy.

Save the ones you love best.
Save the ones you despise.
Saving is an active participation.
The last bus leaves in two minutes.
Don't care if you lost the ticket.
Ride on my lap.
Tell me any lies you can manage.
It'll be a long trip
and I always do enjoy a good fictive yarn.
As long as I care enough about you
to let you turn my page.

There's a Name for It

There's a name for the horror trembling in the corner.
It came to town looking to be understood and loved,
but something in the drinking water brought the worst out of it.
The worst has been getting a lot of grim news lately.
Bernie took the worst to the cleaners
and the worst wasn't even dirty.
The worst's wife ran off and joined the Bobby Jindal Flea Circus.
The horror should admit its worst.
The pros could then examine it under their cosmological bifocals.
They might discover a cure.

There's a name for the cure whimpering in the other corner.
It came to town looking to be loved and understood,
but something in its food brought the sadness out of it.
The sadness has been getting a lot of death threats lately.
Nobody really appreciates its clothing
and it wasn't even dressed.
The sadness should go to rehab.
The amateurs could then massage its open wounds.
They might meet a healing.

There's a name for the healing stuck in the middle of all the rooms.
It came to all the towns and cities looking for lovers who understood.
The few that were found
seemed dazed, and their schoolbooks talked in languages
that broke before they reached the ear.
There's a name for everything, I suppose,
no matter what part of the room you bump into it in.
I'd like to share that name with you,
but when it whispers it to me,
my hearing aid disintegrates.

God Has a New Seating Plan and It Sort of Goes Like This Rag

God has a new seating plan.
Your asses will behave.
Chauffeur-inspired limousines
crash through the in-betweens.
The turkeys get to shove Sarah Palin into the shredder.
Gold will be rediscovered
in Dick Cheney's fangs.
The small miracles of the moment
will spend slow-paced nights
in hot police stations
named after dogs that got famous
in Hollywood.

God has a new girlfriend.
The society pages can't spell her name.
I saw an old movie late last night
in which she made love to a baby elephant
who had a bad drinking habit.
I wish I could explain the new phone book to you
when you demand I spell my name.
All the money is in the drawer.
The natives they get a tad restless.

God told me an adult story.
My ears saw red.
The lights go around and around.
One day, they do find you.
Bring your toothbrush.
Get ready to shine.
The world just broke even,
snapped its vertebrae.
Hey, baby elephant,
lemme see your bottle.
God said, I'll be your designated driver,
the car just won't budge.

Tell All Your Vagrants It's Time for Them to Come Home

Some swear they meant to do good work.
They swear this all day and night.
The walls grow tired and uncomfortable from all their swearing.
Some swear they didn't mean a thing,
they just happened to be wherever they were
when everything came tumbling down.
I used to be more adept at the rigors of tumbling.
Now my legs refuse to obey just any old order.
The premature revolutionary of my bone structure, I guess.
Some stand huge and make it difficult for the light to work.
Some are so tiny I can't discern their rhythm,
even through a magnifying glass.

Days and nights are wary of their shopping lists.
You still can forget all the so-called good things if you're
too much in a hurry.
Tell all your vagrants
it's time for them to come in
out of the fear
and gnarly weather.
Tell the hard room
it's time to attempt a softer tone.

The world claims it doesn't need anybody.
It makes a muscle and dares you to sass it.
Every few seconds the world went to make its favorite muscle,
but something popped,
now it's gone and embarrassed its orbit.
The self-proclaimed gurus can't enunciate their wise riffs.
The watercooler won't cool off.
It's getting so tense
the cops begin making citizen's arrests on themselves.

Maybe the circus will make a vital comeback.
Maybe the animals will talk to us again.
I sit in the cold.
I teeter in the heat.

I mumble valedictions
that can't even sing.
Tell the boys in the back,
as soon as I clarify my front,
I'll be over
for a game of chance.

The gods all fight over the one remote.
It's too difficult to control the TV otherwise.
Send out for the brunch special that will save us.
Pour something sustainable over my confused head.
Tell the powers that be
that the power just might come back on
in a couple of years
if we learn how to behave toward each other.

The oldest man in the universe
chain-smokes old books that everyone knows the endings of.
The youngest girl in the world
rubs her tummy whenever another war breaks out.
Together they boogied across the shrapnel and the rhetoric.
I might be their love child.
I live in a happy sack.
You can tote me to your next big epiphany.
I won't talk out of turn.
The turnstile keeps forgetting which way to go.
Tell mama and papa
I really intended to clean up my act
but the water keeps rising
even if you've already bathed.

Some claim they know where to strike gold.
Some claim they're on a first-name basis with what's-his-name.
I hope they can find their bedroom at night.
I hope they understand the matinee.
Some tell me they know just what I need.
I begin to let the cat knead them.
I don't know where the cat came from.
He just appeared on a whim.

Whims can be quite mirthful, at times.
Mirth told everyone it was going to have a good time.
Good time said if you take your shoes off
you can stay awhile.
The lonesome music
it suddenly gets me making noise.
Maybe all my teeth ran away,
but my gums
sure get moronic with life
just about
this
time
of the
year.

Boulevard Stop

A country full of lost strays
just moved into the vacant apartment in my head.
They all seem way too familiar for my own good.
My own bad gets its pilot picked up.
All the actors in the world and then some
tear my furniture apart looking for their sides.

Mr. Rhythm and Mr. Blues
claim they will assist you in your court case.
The judge wears headphones.
The bailiff has radiation to sell.

Let me out at the boulevard stop.
I hear the drinks there can take you to easy rooms
in which the wallpaper won't slice your retina.

My country got its distemper shot.
It limps back and forth across my spine
trying to remember its PIN number.

When the smoke goes home,
when the screaming goes to sleep,
count your toes
count my toes
count your blessings.

Sometimes those blessings leave home without it.
They get pulled over.
They get jacked up.

When the bloodhounds lose the scent,
when the deaths never get avenged,
make sure you've got your keys.
Lock the door if you need to.

It'll all come headfirst through your favorite window
when the pain plants its flag and says, eureka!

When the lost and found disappears,
count the number of stars looking down at you from the sky,
count your change.

Pick me up at the boulevard stop.
I got a brand-new sack of oft-told stories.
I got a one-way mirror that never thinks twice.
I got a personally autographed headshot of Jesus.

The conference which will decide our fate
takes place in an executive washroom
living in a condemned building
at the edge of something scary.

When the band hocks its instruments,
when the renegades surrender,
when the negotiation gets lockjaw,
it's time to take those sick days,
it's time to make that move.

The van that'll move us is full of blessings
and an arsenal that never says no.
The barking dogs want something stronger than a biscuit.
They want in on the joke.
Go on, toss them the punch line.
Show them you truly care.

Hard Road Claims You Gave It the Soft Shoulder

The noted poet is getting paroled this morning,
too long imprisoned in his worldview.
The dogs and cats are wary
when you suggest they form a more perfect union.

Hard road just called collect,
demands to know why you gave it the soft shoulder.
Such tense days like these
snapping at one's heels.

The warm-up band just went missing in action.
Might have been the inaccurate weather report
gave them false confidence.

You and I just might have to work this room all by ourselves.
Don't unglue,
the walls might ramble on for years,
but an exit strategy just wobbled in, a bit drunk.

The noted poet pulls out his hair.
He tosses it all up at the zealous sun.
Make me quotable, he yells,
and the armies of all the warring nations
begin to recite his work
as they gut one another
in the name
of a higher
love.

The I Love You Gang Is Out of Control

The navel of the Attorney General went mad this morning . . .
No, strike that. The navy of the Attorney General
went mad this morning . . . A huge navel orange squished
the Attorney General this morning . . . No, forget that . . .
bring in the French actresses.
They will clarify this whole mess.
Get Uncle Biscupid's fiddle down at the pawnshop,
I feel like rolling in some hay.
What's that? They don't do surveys anymore here?
Let me read you my list.
Make it Navel. E, not an a. Hold on, the gunman needs
encouraging, come in here and take a look at
this first edition I found in the dumpster:
The I Love You Gang Is Out of Control.
They love you, they love me,
they love anything you can throw their way.
Get me Anna Magnani.
Don't care if she's left this Earth.
I like her energy.
Hold on, darling,
got a call coming in
off some obscure highway
where the traffic does handsprings.
Come on, baby,
we've seen enough video of the Western Front, 1944.
Let's put the dancing light on
and shake it.

There's This Fire Burning Out of Control

There's this fire burning out of control.
It needs some friends and a place to stay.
It used to know how to get out of bed,
but now the bed doesn't want to cooperate.

There's this strange race of people
living inside people who claim I want to know them.
I'd take them up on their offer,
but the stairs go on and on and on.

There's this brand-new planet
rummaging around in my dumpster.
I think it needs a viable lost and found,
maybe it could use a drink.

There's this large bottomless hole in the holy ground.
People smile and throw themselves into it.
There must be something enviable on the other end:
a good book you can't put down,
people able to love.
I hope so, anyway.

The cops pull me over.
Are you him, they ask?
Depends on what you need, I say.
Do you need me to be him?
Whoever him is.
We mistook you for something durable,
they answer, and speed away.

I think I'll go down to the anything-goes room,
I never have to get claustrophobic there.
They got a strong house band.
The service, at times, actually works.

I think I need to sing something.
There's a fire burning out of control.
It asks me to give it a lift into town.
Sorry, I'm on foot myself.
I'm always under somebody's feet.

There's a house of magic around the next bend.
It'd love to ask you in on a first date
but foreclosure signs wave through its hair.

There's a planet knocking on my door.
It wants to sell me something helpful
but all the help got let go,
an economy move.

There's a desperation in the health food.
There's a sadness in the baton twirler.
Pease send your checks to . . .

There's a way to make your way.
There's a cold front in the hot time in the old town tonight.
Take all the time you need when you get up.

I'm sticking around for a few thousand hours,
my work never gets done.
I never know what I'm supposedly doing.
My sheet music is glued together.
I can still improvise, though.
I can still mangle a tune with the best of them.

There's a fire burning out of control,
it needs sustenance, it needs love.
If you can take the heat, come and fetch me,
we'll do this thing together.

It won't be pretty,
it won't really fit,
but that's okay with me.
We are lopsided warriors of we'll try anything once.

Hand me your busted dobro.
I'll let you lead.
It'll certainly be a mess.
Nobody's perfect.
There's a fire burning out of control,
but baby, we just snagged its oxygen.

Import Some Importance from the Big City of Dreams

Don't drive upside down,
they got laws hanging around in the furtive
ends of the dark parking lot.
There's bewildered weather on the way,
any way will do.
Import some importance
from the big city of dreams.

I lost myself there once
on a lark.
Nobody really found me.
I held my identity in so long
I turned blue.

The wild guess pool
will let you swim in its shallow end
if you tip the pistolero good.

The Fractured Committee for Realigning Awry Constellations
just got stuck in an elevator
that can't make up its mind
what floor show it wants in on.

All the Saddle Tramps Sing *Pagliacci*

Hootenanny finds your hiding place,
pulls you out into the sun by your right arm.
You'd rather dig more deep.
Hootenanny hands you a wicked shovel.
Get to it.

Mankind flosses.
Keep the bacteria at bay.
Smile for the history books.
What? You forgot about the history books?
They got shelves of them waiting for your name.

Lady Luck wants to bring down the ticket price:
the scalpers, the rage . . .

Walter Brennan sings *Pagliacci*.
All becomes clear.
Today, the nation that is you
declares a holiday.

Do This One Thing

Do it today, tomorrow, some place shakily in between.
Do it standing, sitting, or in a sad room that hovers over your heart.
Do it as if you knew how.
Do it even if you don't know what the fuck it might turn out to be.
Do it for your favorite pet,
I know you say you hate everything,
but I saw how that creature lights its eyes on you when you come
tearing up the place.
Do it for Granny and Gramps and the Lost Boys and God and the Devil
and all other sultry vacation spots that
claim they know where you live.
Do this one thing and then go off and die quiet.
Do it for the boys, do it because the girls need it,
do it in your shower and bath,
do it on Monday because that's the hardest day of the week
to get the juices roaring.
Do it in the summer, do it when the snow comes.
Do it on spring's first day of parole.
Do it to impress your loved one.
Do it to show folks you now can hate just as easy as them.
Do it when you sleep,
doctors attest it keeps you younger if you do it when you sleep.
Do it when the insomnia grabs hold and won't cut loose,
it gives you something to focus on during all those
hallucinatory waking hours.
Do it for the Gipper, and the Gypper, and the Gypsies, and the Lip Synchers.
Do it for the Grim Reaper, the Pie-Eyed Piper, Godzilla, and
Little Bowl-Overed Peep.
Do This One Thing and the locusts will let your crops slide.
Do it because it's the right thing.
Remember the right thing? It once paid rent in the back back back room.
Do it because if you don't do it,
the howling banshees won't let you in the sweet club.
Do it as if you cared.
A thousand minutes ago you might have been able to pull that one off.
Do it because your neighbor seems to be having fun doing it.
Do it because your neighbor tried it and it hurt bad and you really
never dug him all that well.

Do it because if you don't get it done
it'll keep eating little bits and pieces of your dinner.
Remember well the fleeing days and nights
of wholesome home-cooked anything.
Count the haphazard blessings on a few fingers of one hand.
Do it because the Earth just called you collect and said if you don't
it's gonna commence to shake.
Do it for Tiny Tim Cratchit . . . he grew up, imported England at
the point of a gun, and all the sad lonely people
just got smaller.
Do it for Count Dracula.
He's got a blood disease and all the concerned ladies are
sleeping in all day and have strange-looking hickies.
Do it for the Joads.
They still are trying to find the real Hollywood.
Do it for Gilligan and the Skipper,
that island did something amiss to their constitution.
Do it for anybody passing through.
More and more rootless people are filling the highways
with their zombie shuffle.
Do it in your best go-to-meeting suit.
Do it in the shower,
you can do it easy there,
let it all evaporate,
all the crud you collect into your soul.
Do it for Persephone, Ariadne, Albion, Nicodemus, and Rags.
You don't know anyone with those names but you just love
the way they sound when you speak them.
And finally,
just possibly,
do it for yourself.
Kick out all the specious middlemen,
interpret the ashes and coffee grounds all by your lonesome,
you came into this dance on your own two feet,
supposedly,

and that's how the exits have designed themselves.
Do it because you still seemingly can.
Isn't it grand that you can still function?
The days of entropy are rooted deep now.
The machinery sets to rust rather fast.

Do it because it needs you to do it.
When you're all done,
and it might take some time to get it done,
when your bones are so tired anything makes them giggle,
come to me
and show me your teeth,
and I will ask your hand in
humanity.
I know it'll be difficult,
really it's the most simple thing a person could hope for,
but the simple things sometimes are just too damn difficult
for a person buried in their head.
When it's done being done by you,
come on over and rest up for years.
We'll fabricate some whopping wonders,
we'll revise the contours of history's sheets.
Do it with one shoe on,
don't really need to know which.
Do it barefoot,
as the earth beneath you
disappears out of spite.
Do it with a vital song in your spirit.
All the music critics are locked up in a tower now.
Don't be shy, afraid, too self-conscious.
Do it and
I'll come running
with the iodine, bandages, revival tent, homegrown
you bet, and some coffee that's two inches
south of pure ecstasy.
Do it and I will finally know your name.
And even if you forget yours,
I'll still know the skin you
call home.

We'll Be Seating You Shortly

There's a hole in every magazine.
I guess if we climb into them,
we'll become photogenic and what's going on . . .
We'll be seating you shortly,
the executioner's pale aide promised,
but he kept sneezing
whenever the UFOs flew by.

There's a way of life
in every gas station bathroom,
all you need to do is remember the lost art
of how to believe.
The coyotes meet for drinks just about now.
They got some stories, I bet.

I saw the marching band,
it was in flames.
Somebody complained about the cold.
They have a very adept wordsmith
at the end of the road.
He'll beat his chest,
roar down the law.
Every time he opens his mouth
another mortgage forecloses.

We'll be fitting you soon,
the scorpion's favorite tailor grinned,
in something musical maybe,
in something that will float.
The Big Muddy is getting a rise out of the way you do your business.
The guardian angels are having a devil of a time
trying to keep up.

If Luca Brasi still sleeps with the fishes,
us Pisces should still be very happy.
The tall monuments are afraid of mice.
They shriek and shrink in their presence.
We'll be sending you a car in a few seconds.

Get your last will and testament in order,
your big scene is coming.
The director has made the changes you demanded.

In a tiny cave
at the end of the longevity road,
somewhat wiseass men sit and contemplate the insanity
that is the universe.
One begins to speak backward.
One begins to somersault through fire.
They'll be over soon
for the final episode of *Big Love.*
They can't get enough of Mormon angst.
As one of these intellects chuckled once
to a passing fancy,
Mormon angst is just as valid as anyone else's.

The posse just hobbled back.
They left at a gallop,
but the road has its tricks and turns.
They're covered in dust
and you can't tell anybody from anyone.
Let them get some rest
before you demand their accounting.
In fact, tear up all the accounts.
They never explained all that much
anyhow.

There's a village idiot in every thought process.
Be kind to the one living in your brain's apartment.
Get to know him, or her.
Actually, they are very pleasant
if you overlook some of the horror
they've planted in the garden.
I sense weather coming
that cannot be refused admittance.
We'll be turning you inside out
soon.

Relax, chew on something
resonant.
The invincible hordes
were always nothing but
wimps
who knew how to play with
mirrors.

There's This Hole, See . . .

There's this hole, see,
and it opens up every time you need.
They got great late-night movies
starring eternal actors
who fell over dead
just when the good part.

There's this crisis, see,
and it knows your private number.
I wish God was a number,
we'd smoke him to the end.

There's this war, see,
and it eats red apples
and tells everyone to bypass red meat.

There's this hotel, see,
and the desk clerk ate my shoes.
The bus claims it's too crowded
and the chanteuse got lockjaw.

There's this hole, see,
and it's calling
in all the languages
you swore
you'd
forget.

Attention, Your Humanity Is Showing

Stop feeling other people.
Stop caring. Stop loving. Stop believing.
Become a zombie.
Become ruthless.
Become mean.
You will live forever.
You will go on and on and on,
stomping and chewing and eating,
and all will acknowledge how tall you shine.
Ruthless people bore the shit out of me.
They have nothing left to explore.
They wrote their own book so well
only they can open it.
Feel other people and feel the death that grants you life.
Care. Love. Believe.
Even believe in disbelief.
We won't go anywhere forever,
but it doesn't mean we are anyone the less.
Ride then the slow language
of stumble and miscue.
Ride then the hot pain afternoon
where the band is bent over backward
with becoming.

Nobody Supposedly Gets Out Alive

It's that tired time again.
Count the dead as they are driven to your safe haven.
Glad to see you're still in the game, kid, I'm told.
Just what is the name of this game? I ask.
Stay alive.
Oh, I know that one,
it comes in a beautifully wrapped box.
Be careful when you tear off the paper:
you'll get cut.
Ever since God put everyone on Coumadin,
you got to be careful about getting nicked.

James Dean asked if he could give me a lift.
I felt like walking that day.
Please save the whales.
I'm asked to deny Ahab a spare key.
The new hit show Bowling for Lovers
apparently is scripted.
The bachelor leaps into the big fiery pit.
All drunks everywhere enlist.
It's the beauty of the flag.

Nobody supposedly gets out alive,
I am warned, as I get my ticket punched.
Oh, I mutter, there are ways.
One of those ways crawled across the floor.
Would you like me to play the mandolin, now? it wondered.
I picked it up and drank it slow.
The dust storms are being admonished for illegal motion.

Brace yourself, baby.
The new book that claims it spelled our names right
just can't get up any steam past page one.
Come on down when you're done testifying.
I know what you like to dance to.
My stereo is crazy these days,
but when you waltz through the door,
its medication will take effect.

Hang in there, love.
The Dark Ages are attempting a major comeback.
They're shooting for a long Broadway run.
We'll have to consider the cost of a ticket.
Maybe we'll have it party in our parking lot.
Invite the maimed, invite the forgotten and lost.
I remember their faces as we took showers.

Hold onto your heart, my friend.
The vulnerable stairs keep getting slippery.
Surgery cannot afford us.
Nobody really lives forever,
my bartender says,
and pours me a glass that never ends.
When I get finished drinking it
I'll be up,
maybe in tiny pieces,
but you can handle it.

The hard days crawl quietly off into a corner.
We'd like a little soft now and then.
Death wanders the lobby.
It's read every available magazine.
Someone jump on the table
and belt out a number.
Okay,
I'll do it,
I've got nothing to lose.
I gave it all up at the door.
I toss myself into the frying pan.
It feels kind of edible.

I begin to name the Seven Dwarves.
My memory fails me before I get to the end.
Come on, run and get Snow White.
She'll be coming out of her coma about now.
We'll need her on the dance floor.
Someone run and get Warren Oates, too.
He never really died.
He rides horses in my bloodstream.
He grins, and the sun says,
I think I'm home.

The Day the Whistle Stop Stopped Whistling

Someone forgot to return the overdue ledger,
all that accountability that hemmed and hawed.
History writes checks that bounce.
The right to remain sick is an active verb.
Senators drivel in the loges of the adult movie theater.
Call for any benefactor that remains lucid.

The bag of marbles forgot how to marvel.
The whistle stop can't remember which tune to whistle.
Somebody pull a rune out of the ruins.
Glenn Beck wept and said, I'm Spartacus,
then went roaming through rat's alley
looking for the golden wedge of cheese.

Sarah Palin siphons oxygen from giddy yeti.
All that altitude will eventually kill you.
Come and attempt to balance the sinking ship.
We'll play shuffleboard on the dark side of the moon.
Remain calm as upheaval is born.
Tell the arresting officer you already gave.

Mansions of cardboard
pieces that ate
the smoking gun in Act One
become the theater's new clothes.
Sway a while.
Tell the guillotine to shave a few points.

Unmitigated Shit Hallelujah Choir Hoedown
Sorority Scandal Blues

Virgin Mary just took a lie detector test.
Rush Limbaugh had proof she wasn't a virgin.
He stained himself in adverse anticipation.
His microphone electrocuted itself.
Makes you want to find the best motherfucking wave,
even if you wouldn't know a surfboard from an ass.

The crazy folk come out at night.
They've read the notices.
Makes you need to come up
with a much easier
getaway plan.

Monkey used to once in awhile see.
Monkey today damn well sure do.
Unmitigated shit hallelujah
choir hoedown
sorority scandal
blues
all over your best-dressed suit.

Call for the guys who can handle the net.
Call in the reserves.
The navigation book just threw up.
I guess we won't have lunch there again.
I saw a long tall movie.
All the actors in it were hard to see.
I moved into the front row
and never needed to hear from myself
again.

No No No No . . .

No no no no,
everyone says today.
What did I do?
What did I say?
My left leg fell into a bear trap
but no bears ever come around anymore,
ever since the disaster that befell . . .
You remember the bad blood,
the strange looks,
the nervous air.

No no no no,
the cockroach told the disinfectant.
Everyone wants to live a lot longer.
Some of these fools want to live forever

No no no no,
Forever screams,
you can't move in here,
there's only enough room for me.
You still have the phone number of Mister Smooth?
I need to get some advice.
My hair's constantly packing a suitcase,
threatening to leave,
my stomach doesn't play the stock market very well,
and the avian way is for the birds.

No no no no,
the queen's neck told the guillotine,
come back later,
after the big closeout sale is over.
The Darkness is coming over for tea.
The children done forgot their behavior.
Make mine a double, but leave six of them sitting on the bar.

No no no no,
the prey told the predator,
you simply can't mean it.
If you eat me
you won't be able to experience me.

Oh oh oh oh,
sang the predator,
I will always have fond memories of you,
my sweet prey.

Hey hey hey hey,
come back much later, everyone and everything.
I need to fill my soul's tank.
I'm not very good.

No no no no,
the fire sale told the pyromaniac.
Watch it all go up in smoke,
watch the whole thing float,
the best-laid plans of mice, of men,
of all whistle stops between.

No no no no,
said the yes-men.
They said it so well,
I'll just have to
take them
up
on
it.

Pretty People's Paranoid Party

The pretty people are making noise in the carport.
They are making noise about being afraid of noisy people.
Pretty people are nervous when noisy people exist.
They have met in the carport to eradicate all noisy people.
I look in the Yellow Pages under Eradicate,
find the reliable number of a pair that eradicates noisy people.
I run out and throw the phone book at the pretty people.
Here's your way out, now shut up and let me chill out.
The pretty people get upset by my tossing the phone book.
They call me uncouth.
They probably got that right.
Never had much couth.
Couldn't tell you what it looked like, what it ate.
The cops finally cop, make the pretty people move on.
The ugly people are waiting their turn.
They've been waiting patiently.
Something about that carport attracts all kinds.
The ugly people congregate.
They talk so quietly it's downright eerie.

The Man with the PhD in Eating

The man with the PhD in eating
sits in the forbidden corner of a very popular restaurant
eating anything and everything
they put in front of his face.
He ate the Kingdom of Suck My Sweat,
all 14,568 inhabitants.
I was gonna maybe move there.
Heard the rent was cheap
and the nightlife never slept.
He eats and eats and eats.
The firemen nervously await the day he explodes.
I looked at this guy for awhile,
but it got way too obvious.
You can eat your way through any and every thing,
but sometimes you just don't have any goddamn
taste.

Sayings

The sayings that supposedly save us
now say they have nothing to report.
Rewind your life
back to when the lights worked
and the maintenance guy
actually maintained pretty damn good.
If the heat keeps rising,
you might want to calmly move your
worldview a few feet.

Sayings pile up by the emergency exit,
another fire hazard.
Have you heard this one?
A lonely guy discovers that humans
embrace solitude as a defense mechanism
that never fails to impress.
When you go it alone
the only consistent argument
is easily won.
Can't actually claim who wins it, though.
You or yourself.
Some days there are miles and miles
of untested road
between the two.

Lately all would-be debutantes
are trained for guerrilla tactics.
Those guerrillas often are mistook for big apes.
Nobody has a kind word lately for apes, big or small.
They've outstayed their arbitrarily agreed-upon duration.
Big apes aren't adept at sayings.
They make loud obvious noises with their lips.
Small apes want to somehow pretend they're chimpanzees.
Chimpanzees are really good at deciphering sayings.
They fling their shit at the relentless sun
and by their flinging
words of wisdom form and you finally
understand your path in life.

My path in life
steered good-natured off the track of beaten.
You don't want to stay beaten too long
or you grow ossified.
Ossify and Harriet
were America's favorite surrogate parents
until their sayings
flooded reality
and the fact checkers drowned.

Fact checkers once ran chubby
but the famine came calling
and the famine was full of resonant sayings
that lured the ear's ability to know better
down a dark one-way street.
The dark one-way streets once had style,
now they meander and grow trite.
Trite tried to remain a vital force in world literature.
Giant shelves grew fat and sloppy with trite.
Trite put out quarterly books of sayings,
but their sayings ate themselves and
nobody could hop on one foot after
reading them.

Hopping on one foot is illegal
in some parts of the brain.
Can't begin to tell you in just what parts.
Maybe in part four.
Part four always sounds good.
Part four is full of sayings that make you tingle.
Do you remember what it takes to tingle?
Certainly not a college degree.
The college got the third degree
and is now deathly afraid of anyone in a uniform.

Uniforms all got colds
and they can't sing at the big rally as planned.
The big rally wants to say something profound
but profound is unconscious in the lost
and found and the only person who can revive it is

a chimpanzee pretending to be an ape,
and he's too busy pretending to
pay attention to his bag of sayings,
which is now blowing all over the
main drag that was going to escort us out of this furnace
and into some specious safety zone.

Specious safety zones have been rezoned so far out,
none of us
in our minds,
right or other,
shall ever
make it.
Make it to the big soirée,
the last saying
says,
and you reach deep deep deep down
into your soul,
what's left of it,
looking for that big soirée,
and all you find
is just one more
big ape
who has this very funny
saying
on the tip of his teeth.
Go big ape,
say say say,
deep deep deep down,
below the marrow's white flag,
say who and what you are,
say your name four times
and watch the
shit
fly.

The Maniac in the Engine

There's a maniac in the engine.
It wants so very hard to love you,
but love got illegal in the days and nights of fear.
Everyone traded their hearts in for guns that worked.

There's a world inside the trash.
It wants so very hard to make it home,
but the road back got torn up by too much stress.
Everyone stood in line for Thomas Brothers Guides that were legible.

There's a sickness in the remedy.
There's a deafness in the hearing aid.
Someone get up on the bridge and take a good look.
Tell the engine room to behave.
Sometimes your sonar doesn't lie.

There's a fear in the strongman's final muscle.
It talks so musical you can't do anything but give in.
The lonely rooms ask too much rent.
You search your bank account,
but the location's moved away in the night.

The dying-forever twins
have folded up their big tent.
The lion can't roar so good anymore.
A strange planet got caught in his throat.
Pass the wounded gate slow.
Tip the bartender good.
He knows where you cry.

When the hours attempt to brush you off,
when the police escort falls asleep,
learn the new national anthem.
Of my skin, I cringe,
of my mind, I deny.
Go ahead, stand up and sing it.

There's a ghost in the infant.
I don't know if it's benevolent or malignant.
You can't judge a ghost by its aura.
Kings and queens fall to their scraped knees.
They'd love a rematch.
They're sending out for a referee
who supposedly can't be bought.

The maniac in the wedding cake
swears magic is holy.
The heart is an atoll
in some raging sea.
Maybe we'll grow there.
Maybe we'll turn to stone.

Go ahead, then. You can weep for free.
Your tears become lakes
upon which brave men and women attempt to stroll.
We drown by inches daily.
We sing god bless the lost and found.
We throw our hats into the ring.
We throw our towels at the incoming rockets.

Good morning,
I came over to your private war to borrow a cup of sugar.
I really never need it.
I just wanted to read the book of your eyes.
I just wanted to ask you your name.

Be Kind to Monsters Week

It's Be Kind to Monsters Week.
They've been misunderstood and misrepresented for years.
That glib press,
those harsh commentators;
guess their hearts are missing in action.
All the monsters in the world
hire Burson-Marsteller to represent them.
Oprah had a couple of them on her show,
the audience went down on their knees and wept.
One monster wanted to know if I had a teenage daughter.
I sorely disappointed it when I said
I have no teenage anythings.
The only movie theater here in Florence
now has to be monster accessible.
Monsters now get their rents reduced.
I asked a monster if he wanted to watch a Budd Boetticher Western.
It snarled that it didn't like the Western genre.
Somedays you just can't win,
the monsters tire and crawl off to wherever they thrive.
I reach into my own inner monster,
I pet it, say, how you doing tonight, bud?
My inner monster purrs;
it's a hedonist,
and much more important,
loves watching Budd Boetticher Westerns with me.
I love my inner monster.
Do you love yours?
We watch The Tall T.
I swear, Chink, you hit him in midair,
Skip Homeier says.
My inner monster giggles.
All is well in the tottering republic.
All is tenuous, all is viable, all is beautiful.

Oops . . . The Manual

Important-looking guy comes over my TV.
My TV gets all nervous and tense.
I best give it a drink.

Important-looking anyone
jumps up on top of my head.
I pull out my vocabulary cards.
Did you somewhat read your paper?
Did anyone go swimming?

Important-sounding function
just wrote a bad check.
The bank's got a hernia.
They have no suspects.
I best give it a wink.
Never pull rank.

The desert wrote a song.
It sang, I'm wide, vast, and can sing all night.
The bank's got issues.
Calm down,
I see your submarine.
It surfaces when you blush.

Did anyone ask questions?
Did anyone sit in the swings?
I wanna go high,
push it up a notch.
I best give it a rest.

Oops . . . said the manual,
I got lost.
Follow the yellow brick anything.
I think we're there,
in the musician's back room.

Oops . . . the manual gasped,
I forgot my meds.
We all leapt up.
We said
yes.

Please Remove Your Brain in the Presence of a . . .

All the so-called Seven Wonders,
trapped together in a Volkswagen van,
they don't even enjoy one another.
They repeatedly try to out-wonder
each other. Gives a poor idiot like me
a headache. I wasn't made for
this nonsense.

Please remove your brain in the presence of anything
that demands you think much too hard.
Pray that you'll successfully walk away from the police lineup
you're starring in.

About this time of the month
we all begin to resemble each other,
and when we begin to relinquish all rights to
the hungry sociopaths who claim they love us
better than we could ever like ourselves,
it'll be difficult to get the proper residuals to the
right individuals.

I told the frightened people
I'd take point,
but when I went to turn on the light,
the electricity called me a liar
and refused to play fair.

The swing set needs more kick.
The stock-in-trade dangerously calls for replenishing.
The photogenic gamblers are endeavoring to learn new sleights of hand.
Metaphorically inclined men and women
confess they can't understand the fine print on the warranty
that keeps blowing away when you reach for it.

Please remove your nationality in the presence of
a wounded anything.
Pain is assuredly worldwide
and easily ingested without language.

Those Seven Wonders were slightly overrated.
Their managers had done too well with the press clippings.
Maybe, though, we'll still get a full house
for the next show.

Maybe it's time to unveil the renegade new Eighth Wonder.
It keeps on ticking no matter how many times you feel you've successfully killed it,
and just how important or long-lasting is death these days
anyway?
So many people seemingly embrace it with passion.
The museums are overfilled with newly minted corpses.

Tell my server I'll figure what I'll order
as soon as I clear my throat.
Too many misplaced dreams are caught inside it,
making it very difficult for me to
chime in when
my part
rears its ugly head.

Just Might

The large wound in Santa Claus
just might prevent Christmas
from staying out
of the new super-deluxe downtown jail
that just landed.
Arguments climb aboard our blood,
tell us this just might be the way.
It ought to be.
Never believe it
when they tell you such stuff.
Lovers supposedly withstand
all ornery weather.
I got a lunchpail
with such vision embedded in its skin,
just might be the dance
everyone's been dying
to learn.
Raise the legs of hope
above the ever-rising fire.
Just might be the very thing,
indeed,
to see you home
safe,
through wary evening
and tense morning.

Santa recovers,
lowers his gun
for now.
The dance
takes a much-needed rest.
Somebody invents magic.
We drink it,
toast one another
as the artillery signs its autograph.

Come Hither, Come and Yawn

The church went out of business.
They had a going-away party.
We all got green at six.
Teach bingo callers new tricks.
Come hither, little lady,
come and yawn.

Precipice got the flu.
You size some graphs.
A midget sees way too much
when he's a king of the clouds.
The front row melted.
The pianist lost a shoe.
I think I'll take regular coffee.
The firing squad will send you off soon.
Come slither, come upon.

The sun goes where it wants.
I've seen the clues
do the Melting Swahili,
do the Dick Nixon Shoe.
A midget sees way too much
when you run your projector this low
in the small houses that haven't been named.
Come blister, come beyond.

The front row will now go last
and the hearing aids, they will all know
everything you say
goes through one ear.
That's when the curtain comes up.
The sun burns you when it wants.
God ran into a leper.
The leper sang God a song.
God's face got red,
and jazz was born.

one last round

One Last Round

One last round for the missing links
and their eager fans,
stranded on the dark side
of the anything goes.

One last set of instructions
that'll see you safely home,
even if the lunatics took over
the wilderness and rebuilt it to
claim your every move.

Take the burning train home to the origin of jazz.
Tell all your friends you expect to sidestep the bullet.
One last round for the lost and never truly found.
They walk around in circles in the middle of the square,
humming old doors with locks that have seen better days.

I was whispering my name to semicoherent seagulls
when the lights all rudely came on.
I better go and see if my good profile
is out of bed just yet.

One last round for all the nondrinkers.
They've climbed aboard the shore they felt was due them.
They lay on the beach
counting the holes in the sky,
which all the civilizations
disappeared through.

One last round
and then the ogre gets the girl.
She should relax:
he's a pretty decent guy
as ogres go.
When he smiles,
the dead rise
and begin to glow.

Fly Away the Night

Sometimes you reach for the stars
and come up with your palm covered in shit.
Don't fret.
All fertilizer is welcome by the Earth.
Rub your hand in the consciousness of the Earth.
Tell the avenging tribunal you're past all recrimination.
Let the screaming custodians of what passes for the norm
tire from overexercising.
They will collapse on the neutral street.
You might get a blanket to cover them come the cold times.

Fly away with me tonight.
I have no destination in mind.
My wings are subject to ornery implosion.
Doesn't matter if I plummet.
They tell me my head at times can be resilient,
when I want it to be.

Fly away with no landing strip anywhere.
Free-falling is valid self-expression.
Sometimes you hold your head in your hands.
You offer it to the leader,
whatever that might be.
The leader can't be bothered.
So much work left wherever you stumble.
More often than not you hold your heart in your hands.
You offer it as a sacrifice to the hungry board of trustees.
But haven't you heard?
They're all dieting this week.

Hang onto your heart a bit longer,
you'll need it come morning.
There's a dance hall opening in every 10th man and woman
that claims the 9 ahead of them could be family
of some obstreperous kind.
Sometimes you think the quicksand is sucking you in way too slow.

You get bored with the whole process,
but just before nodding off
a rope finds you
and you pull yourself back onto your fine fine horse.

Fly along this odd circumference.
Tell the sharpshooters their ammo
won't sing in key anymore.
The rainbow ahead no doubt is an illusion,
but magic always had its way with us.
Maybe down the line,
some years hence,
we'll make that all-important soirée,
but in the meantime,
there's more than enough room in the parking lots
of the dispossessed
to strut our ways and means.
Let me see your best profile.
You can rub my belly.
If anyone complains too loud,
we can tear the hearing aids out of our souls.

Slaughterhouse Cathedral

The dead wake up hungry.
They'd like their rights reread.
In between the cracks of the small print,
something claimed it hurt.
The specialists glowed green in the dark of the operating room.
Magicians found their hands cemented in their hats.
Round up your hungry.
Shake the can of bug spray.
Something weird just happened.
Normalcy went up in flames.
Tell the delivery man,
please don't be too late.
They need us for something vital,
but it's so easy to lose your parking space.
They're screaming in general admission
about wars and treaties and what happened to the dog's leash.
The ogres are in town
looking for hot dates.
Gimme a sax.
Gimme a spoon.
I want to hear Billie Holiday karate chop foreign devils.
In Slaughterhouse Cathedral,
every conquered nation
is underage.
Bring your selected, collected poisons.
I'll bring what's left of me.
We'll go around and around
until one of us takes a fall.
Maybe we'll both go down
together.
The dead wake up ornery.
Their damn eggs are burned.
In between the retreating armies
and the slipshod sun,
I see you looking
right back at me.

Your eyes might be poems I'll never understand,
but baby,
frankly
it's been one hell
of
a
read.

Say No Goodbyes in Languages We Forgive But Forgot

Paint won't stop congealing.
Tired guard holding up the gate can't pronounce my name.
Maybe that meteor shower will finally land a job.
They got a special gym just for soothsayers.
Those soothsayers need to lose a whole lotta something that could
be weight.
The pet psychic on the Animal Planet cannot fathom Bob the Cat,
'cause he knows better.
Triumphant baked goods fall from some champagne-chaperoned sky.

What I meant by he knows better is Bob the himself cat,
not the pet psychic.
Someone grab a minuet and let it unfold.
I will take the lady dancing on some hot planet
where the string section sleeps at the foot of hummingbirds.
They will close off the final escape hatch sometime next week.
The Governor himself will be coming down for it.
Put your everloving arms around this tired boy's neck.

Cajun music on every tongue,
Say No Goodbyes in Languages We Forgive But Forgot,
take the gent dancing on some woodsmoke.
Daylight slowly walks up the aisle
to accept its award.
Whimsy, please, much much much more of it,
and a sad boy can bounce just as well as the new breed of
unfeeling robots who think they are just so so so immune.

Cajun music in every bone,
someone grab the baton and let her rip.
The final escape hatch just pulled off its mask and
it turned out to be just another open door.
No evil bad monster out there,
just a whimpering little stupid lost ornery fool.
You could go barefoot across the firing squad's pedigree.

Cajun music will get you sung,
and a sad boy can take it just as well as the sad girl.
Together they built a rest stop for poets,
right there along the fissure
where the sun kisses the consciousness
and we roll
ever so
heartful.

The Hard Men Are Getting a Tad Soft Just About Now

Come with your clothes on, even.
There's gonna be a laying-on
of hand-me-downs.
Tall ships will finally fit into tiny coves
and grace will be making a comeback
after all these years.

Someone will speechify.
They'll be testifying for hours.
In the rubble of another day
gone to ground,
the hard men are getting
a tad soft
just about now.

Wake up the lunatic sleeping next to you.
The party really can't get going without you both.
They got cracks in the pavement
that you can herd cattle through.

Come with your bulletproof skin,
your cosmic mumbling.
You might have to be chosen.
You might be the one to lead us
around and around and once more around.
We'll all get dizzy from squaring the circles.
The children will all swear you fathered them.

Come with your too-cross-at-times cross to bear.
Everyone will be named before the roof caves in.
Everyone will get their own radio show.
The call letters will try to remember your number.

Come with your Sunday-go-to-meeting blank mystified stare.
The big mystery will be resolved in a few minutes.
Somebody very important will be strutting in soon.
Let the pulled back muscles rejoice.
There's a chiropractor walking on my grave's spine.

Sing one for the very important people.
They're way way overdue.
Their egos overloaded their flight.
They've been misplaced in the sky.
You might have to stand up.
You might have to say no.
They'll be coming at you for miles.

I don't think any of it means much to too many people.
Just have a good time
as they try to twist you inside and out.
It's okay.
Pretzels are fine things,
just don't lay down too much salt.

The hard folks
just can't seem to hold up their end any longer.
Maybe it was way overrated,
their end.
Let it all roll where it will.
The landscape has many addresses.
The hard folks once swore they never cried.
I wish it would stop raining.

And What Does the Dog Have to Say?

The dog's lying bloody and hot on the overrated road.
Ask him what he's got to say
about your condition.
I saw your condition walking across a creaky bridge.
It'd just got a pedicure and manicure.
The dog told me a story
about when you dated the world.
I didn't know what to believe.
I opened the phone book's yellow pages.
Under What to Believe it said,
not so much.
The cat, on the other hand,
never says a thing.
She just stares through all your laws and beliefs.
She's been there and back.
The posse is forming,
this time for real.
They won't be back
without the missing link.
Not too sure if the link is really missing
or just hanging around under an assumed name.
I think it tried to engage me last night
but my head wasn't in town.
My body sort of bumbled its way through.
The dog used to go to a lot of parties
but somehow he got bounced off of all those A lists.
I rub his belly
and epiphany begins to Fats Waller us toward reconciliation.
Pack up your paranoia.
We're reaching the all-inclusive stage.
My blood type can move in with yours.
There will be some knock-down-drag-outs certainly,
but our kids will become character actors,
even if films needing them vanish.
The dog tells me his real name.
It doesn't faze me in the least.

Wang Dang Doodle

If I see you sinking,
I'll throw you my life.
We sort of float dumb.
Wang Dang Doodle
looked us up in the trees.

If you see me shrinking,
save a place in the sack.
When mighty giants fade,
the torn heart still holds.

If you find me at your door,
think twice before making that call.
There are days coming.
There are days that will take you home.

Wang Dang Doodle
ran up the clock.
Sometimes you freeze,
often not.
A hardheaded lover
just hymned a best-selling thing.

Wang Dang Doodle
lives on the porch.
I got some minutes to burn.
Let me shake the country of your hand.

Don't Pull the Earth Out from Under Me
Until I've Had Two More Shots

The end is coming,
Chapter One proudly announced.
Will you be prepared to sacrifice for
the good of the team?
Will the sparrows still return
your investment?
The matron knows exactly which chair will fit you.
Don't go asking too many questions:
the answer lady has arbitrary hours.
The trail of fire
almost got reinstated.
There's a place you can burrow down deep,
make a name for yourself,
haunt all types of imposing houses
with your wailing.
Don't pull the earth out from under me
until I've had two more shots.
The doctor told my sense of balance
to behave.
The tender end of town
just got possessed
by an eerie proclivity to survive at any cost.
Maybe the city fathers
will honor their blood test results.
Put your life in a sturdy mailer.
Send it off ASAP to anyone who could use a laugh.
I'll be finished soon with my homework.
You can have your heart back.
It won't ever be intact
but it will still be able to come running
when the sirens sing
and the pain decides to take a pass.
The light show
will connect up soon.
Don't get ornery if the moon refuses to shine.

Energy conservation is a good thing,
they claim
just before they evaporate.
Come back in a few minutes
if you really need to do the room.
My head's momentarily imploding,
but soon I'll retrace my so-called groove.
All the simultaneous radios
play the same riff.
It has a thousand different titles,
but once you clear the final hurdle
it all goes down in you the same.
Please don't eat the Earth
until you know for sure
you're actually
hungry.
If you feel compelled to devour everything in your path,
how about checking out a nice huge mirror
and commence,
with alacrity,
to gnaw on
the first thing
you
see.

Earful of Sun

How you get up in the early hours
tells me a lot about your dancing ability.
They claim the highway has no best friend.
Someone bailed it out of jail, though, last night.
We sat and drank beer and watched the meteors fall.
I got an earful of sun and had to wash my ears out afterward.
Maybe the resurrection will show up as promised and give us
something to sing about.
Maybe it won't.
I intend to sing anyway.
When you finish reciting all the pain,
when the dog finally digs up his last bone,
come on over and put the bulletproof vest down.
Everybody says they want to be loved.
They say it over and over and over.
As soon as they finish hitting me over the head,
I will get up and love them.

No Heart Attacks at Testimonial Landing

Surely everyone knows you by now.
They have marathons and telethons in your honor.
At least it sounded like your name when I ran through the room.
Is there someone else walking the Earth with your exact name?
When the dog brings in the paper I see your face on page one,
but then maybe it's a clone of your face, I don't know anymore.
You told me you were a very important person and I believe
what you adamantly tell me.
When the phone rings, they ask where you live.
They want to come to you and drink strong Scotch.
I know you are at Testimonial Landing,
working on your acceptance speech.
I really don't have any idea what you are accepting,
but speechwriting is sort of a lost art in this
electronic age.
One of the kids who does odd jobs around this end of things
claimed you looked kind of pale, was worried about
the state of your heart.
At Testimonial Landing there is a sign before you cross the
bridge to get to it that says, no heart attacks need apply
or if they try to, they will be arrested and locked up.
I attempt to walk across the bridge to Testimonial Landing
but splinters get into the soles of my feet
and I keep having to go back to the first aid station
and get them removed.
I should get some shoes soon enough and
then I can come over and see just what the hell is going
on in your life.

Tell the Fear to Come Back Later When
Somebody Is Actually Home

I saw the guy who said he's gonna live forever.
I told him forever didn't mean much to me
unless you could eat it when you were hungry.
He told me to quit being naïve,
made me buy his how-to-stay-healthy book.
I tried to give it my best,
but my best recently is kind of done in by all
sorts of banal things.

The Fear showed up about 11:45 this morning.
It looked like it had one hell of a night.
Its hair was all messed up.
Its suit was all rumpled.
I had a rough road, Fear claimed.
Could you spare me some of your time?
Come back when I'm actually home, I said.
Aren't you home right now? Fear said with a puzzled look.
Looks can be deceiving, I suggested,
shutting the door.
Fear took a piss in my parking lot
then limped off, cursing.

The guy who claimed he'd live forever
just went in for a heart transplant.
The surgical team cut deep deep deep deep
but couldn't find anything.
They'll have to come back after getting a much-needed time-out.

The man who claims he'll live forever
begins to laugh and cry simultaneously.
No mean feat,
it requires dexterity, skill, poise.
Tell everyone to come back, he sings,
once I get home.
It won't be for years.
Don't know what shape I'll be in when I do.
Thankfully a student nurse
who's led one all-too-vulnerable life

grows tired of his laughing and crying.
She gives him a dose of whoopass,
that brand-new controversial medication
that might give you metaphorical side effects.

The guy who intends to live forever
begins to crawl up and down the hospital hallway.
Tell him to come back to his room
whenever he gets home.
The road, it takes its time and toll on you.
You begin sitting remarkably straight behind your wheel,
but by the time you pull up for what's due you
you're hunched way way over and out.

As for naïve me,
I stole a dose of whoopass.
I don't intend to do anything forever,
especially live,
that would be incredibly boring.
I'm gonna go and see if I can find that limping Fear,
see if it ever calmed down after such a hard night.
Maybe we'll grab a bite,
see a halfway accessible movie.

The guy who claims he's gonna live forever
just got a pink slip.
Oh oh, don't mind me,
anything I can do is simply temporary.
I strolled onto this stage unannounced.
I became a part of some attempted scenery.
Maybe you heard me call you.
Maybe you saw through me.
Don't matter much.

You lift up your heart's baggage.
Hope it won't give you bursitis.
Time for me to soirée up the trail.
Maybe we'll connect sometime,
over something edible.
Maybe we'll do a duet
on the side of the deaf highway.

Nobody may hear it
but it'll treat us just fine.

Tell the Fear it can sleep in,
we really won't need it for a bit.
We're on our own.
None of us is all that unique.
None of us really is too serene.
At times we shrug off the burden.
At times we encourage the load.
We're imperfect, unsure dancers
experimenting with the history of foot placement.

Tell the Fear it's really trite in the places it feels it's revolutionary.
Tell it to learn how to stay in the game.
I'll be home one of these years.
I might invite it in for coffee.
My home is whatever I feel.
At times we become ciphers.
At times we become crystal clear.
None of us gets out alive,
said the rock star to the burning comet.
Don't really matter.

There's a soirée in your eyes.
You may not see it.
I hear you humming
beneath the falling objects.
I hear you singing
when your lungs have gone to ground.
Not sure just what ditty you're sharing
but I feel my feet moving
regardless.
Maybe the earth under me is cutting my feet
or just maybe
you've dosed me with whoopass.
It all mounts its horse from the same side.
Here we go,
galloping
in a trotting zone.

When the End of the World Forgets
to Call You on the Phone

The big mistake sits at the corner of the bar,
crying into its beer.
You've been here before
and your bullshit detector is flashing red.
Pity the lynch mob.
They were all set to lay down their fury
but all the trees were missing.
When the end of the world
checks into the hospital
for a couple of controversial yet important tests,
you wait for love to call you,
send you something sweet.
The thermostat actually thinks you're hot,
those revealing high school pictures.
Bleak things eventually fade.
Bring you a big play time.
Strap it to your shin.
Uneasy waters do not go well with prescription meds.
Stir me up, serve me swell,
when the dark army
collapses from too much hate.
The end of the world
used to be represented by better managers.
The elevators get a bit sticky
when you reach for them while asleep.
Better late than never,
unless never only comes once.
Give it lemonade.
Give it love.
The big mistake
has a little tiny heart.
Be careful
when you back up.

The One Road

The one road out of town
keeps coming back for seconds.
Please tell the maestro to conduct himself properly.
Longevity is being treated by the nervous pulmonologist
for its increasing shortness of breath.
For a good time call yourself.
Today is the big day, they say.
Make sure your fingernails are trimmed and clean.
Here comes the ice cream truck.
It only has one flavor left,
but if you choose to use what's left of your outlawed imagination,
it'll taste different every time you bite into it.
Tell the guardian angels
the guardrail is about to snap.
Tell those scraggly scrawny imps
to have the Devil of a time.
The one bathroom left in the world
could use a plumber with wit, style, grace.
Tell Ali Baba
we only have 39 thieves on the active roster.
Cutbacks.
Pain in every window that offers itself for you to peer through.
Everybody claims this week they can sing the blues.
No Brains Billy just formed a band.
He said he saw the elephant.
Did the elephant see him in return?
The elephant denies all.
He's got a big deal in the works.
The one road would like to play some poker with you.
You're such a card.
Please tell Moses the Red Sea should have a part on the right side.
The flying saucers are frustrated,
they keep trying to mate with frisbees.

Don't Miss Too Much What You Never Had

Wake up the dead in a few minutes,
they'll be needed to move on somewhere.
The renovation committee deems it necessary.
Call the rage off due to rain.
Make sure no escapees are under the hood.
It's gonna get somewhat cold tonight.
I saw the cheerleaders freeze
during their most personal favorite moves.

Holy men go sliding upscale.
They skid clumsily into what passes for nirvana.
Their resultant torn shins cause much concern
in the waiting rooms of the mediocre.
Send a clown in just about now,
somebody needs to remember how to laugh.

I got countries in my pockets
that have never been born.
They need to get housebroken
before the next meeting of the coven.

Don't miss too much
what you never had.
The police lineup goes on for miles.
I recognize my better angel in it.
It's getting a bit rank:
too many sudden wake-up calls,
too many leaking fountain pens.

Tell your good time
to stay just a little longer.
There must be something we can wear
that will see us through.
Hold your cup up,
I will pour you a story.
It will quench your fear.

The axe man is just warming up.
The trees we are
bound to fall.
Couldn't tell the furnace from the stove.
Give me a few more minutes.
A giraffe wants to go necking.
I saw the plague
when it crawled out of bed this morning.
It looked kind of pale.
Couldn't remember when it was born.

Don't look for me in the big book of movers and shakers,
I couldn't clear the barbed wire.
Guess I'll sit here on my shrinking bar stool.
The hordes attest they still comprehend advancement,
but they keep revolving in the same door.

Tell the dentist I need more laughing gas,
otherwise the stand-up comic will feel sad.
Move the death ray a little farther from my shadow.
From now on
it's a sing-along.

Homecoming
for MJ Taylor, Home Plate King

Home's coming over.
Home's moving in.
Home knows where you hang.
Home home home on all those ranges.

You've got the range you bet.
You've got the deed in your heart.
Home's coming over to build itself in you.

Sometimes the lonely cold night,
sometimes the lonely cold night wants a home.
Don't mind it too much.
Lonely cold night needs a friend.

Home's en route alright.
Home's about to
move in.

The lights along the highway clarify the skin.
There's a light flickering in the window of the eyes.
There's a light helping all the supposedly lost boats make their way
back to shore.

Home's coming on.
Home's gonna sing your name.
There's an all-night coffee shop in your soul.
All the vulnerable animals and trees come there.

Don't worry about so much.
Home's coming in for a landing.
It knows you're built to last.
It knows you're built for comfort.

The storms come.
Sometimes they even leave.
John Prine told us about those storm windows.
There's a hootenanny in the way you say your name.

There's a hootenanny in your heart
when you sing us your name.

No guarantees ever, said the sign.
Doesn't mean a thing,
just as Woody Guthrie hummed,
turn that sign over.

Hey hey, it says.
Home's settling down in your soul.
Home's got stories to tell your bones.

Home,
don't you know,
is on
a
roll.

The Last Roundup

I met a sobbing one dollar bill
trying to make sense of all its change.
An informed man or woman could massage
its tortured muscle.

The Last Roundup seeks agile
people for a sustaining relationship.
Maybe not everyone truly requires splints.

Last night it was difficult to enunciate anything.
We all had highlighted speeches,
but stage fright knows more intimate kitchens
than originally surmised.

In the affluent cavern of the banal cadaver
no one will be seated after the first nine minutes.
I'm a doctor, the wind shrieks,
and your skin yells, I'm just another patient.

The Last Roundup spooks very very easy.
Do not attempt to chew gum and confess your undying
love at the same time.

Soon the magic broom shall sweep it all up,
once again clarity will rear its ambiguous face
beneath a sun that at times
can burn right through you
in search of a planet to orbit it,
and at other times
will freeze you out
just when you assumed the pot was yours for the taking.

At the end of the drive
they swear your sheet music will remember you.
We all need
a little swig of empathy
to cut the dust.

Successfully get your heart to market
before the price drops too far down
for the new Recovery Act's terms
to mean anything.

Recuperate in the quiet corner of the melee,
tell the hangman you only have one neck to
give for your country.
You'll do it
in your own time,
and when the Push Comes to Shove Committee
claims it's time to go all out,
explain to them as you give them the boot,
that all out is now very much in,
and the trains run on time okay,
its just that the depots keep moving about
due to restlessness and worry.

Day and Night nervously size up one another,
wondering how much truth there actually is
inside the Cracker Jack box.

The Last Roundup always assumed it was first-born,
that through negligence
the proper order got messed up.

When you hear this line of talk,
you shrug and tell the invaders
that the local turf is way overrated.

Everyone can cry for 15 minutes,
the church bell suggested.
It rang a long long time
but God has call-waiting.

Cough It Up or Die Boogie

The ice cream won't eat us anymore.
It even changes its flavor
as we go to speak.
Cough it up or die,
the undertaker told the unidentified flying object.
The next rest stop
hasn't slept in four days.
I took a quick peek through the big badass telescope.
Everybody was an ant.
There's a house for rent
in the stomach of my mind.
I'll wash all the windows
as soon as I learn to grow up.
Tall men with diplomas made of Silly Putty
blot out the sun.
I was getting sunburned before my time.
Build a city, lock its doors, throw away the keys.
I live in your bathroom.
I dance when it rains.
Cough it up, the queen of everything
told all the court jesters that thrive in me.
Cough it up
and run like hell.
I've seen hell's legs.
They got big and ugly.
It ain't about to run anywhere.
The luxury liner eloped with the gondola.
Guilty as charged, the Supreme Court bellowed.
I'm down to one last check.
One day soon just you watch it bounce.

Get Yourself a Functioning Guru and Avoid Falling Civilizations

The sea serpents will see through your miserable excuse of an ongoing navy.
You won't like what they tell one another about your momma.
Last night the last sane man in the county
imploded all over the major air currents.
I don't think it was really anything he said,
maybe it was his feeble attempt at throwing his weight
around the circumference
of the Earth.

The judge advocate is thawing out the law.
The microwave is too hot so don't take it to the pawnshop just yet.
Lonely gurus seek acolytes in the dollar store.
Avoid falling civilizations,
unless their bark isn't as bad as their bite.
Pull the plugs out of your brain,
time to give a listen.
Tell the whirlwind what your sewing kit intends to reap.
I don't think it was anything I did.
I don't do too much about this time of day.

Doctor said learn to shrug some of this debris off.
Soon the implants will have children.
Cosmology will make a comeback.
I don't think it was anything we ate.
The jury screamed at each other for days,
but when night landed on them
their hearts sang such a painful lullaby.

I'm heading south for the Big Void Conference.
I heartfully accept my inanity.
The top ten Yahoo Google kids
are demanding you stop hitting them,
they need to find where their best profiles went off to hide.
Lemme see how you walk the water,
everybody says it's what you need to do to get by.
Drowning seamen all concur,
too much salt in the diet can lead to severe repercussions.

Tell the lounge act
it better start to roll me soon
or I'm gonna have to fall on my dubious kneecaps
and testify to anything.

Maybe the lunch special will admire our stomachs.
Maybe the condemned man and woman will get a reprieve.
Tell the arresting officer
every blind man can be a solid-enough witness
if you sing to them oh so gentle.
Clean the bleeding carpet.
Dance for God and country.
The convenience store around the corner
swears it was you and nobody else.

Cut the deck and pray the rain won't drink you too quick.
Once upon a time,
a few seconds back,
they discovered gold in the toothless
Book of I Told You So.
If you blend in with the torn scenery,
do it quiet,
all the major participants involved
confess they don't sleep much anymore.

Tell the heat to simmer down.
You me and nobody else.
Do us quiet.
The angry rosary,
nothing but beads of sweat
in a furtive time of incalculable cold.
Stare for years through the haze.
All apparitions ahead could be a rhythmic rest stop.
Perplexed galaxy seeks readable way of life.
Pull your wounded body up onto this tipping-over stool.
Row a confident leaking canoe.

All the warriors have gone hiding
under their wives' skirts.

Leave them there for now,
we got fish frying
on the fevered brain of the world.
Throw your javelin into the sky,
watch it impale the moon.
Tell your watch you just don't have the time,
not enough hours in a century.
Can you yodel?
They got schools that will show you the way.
Just put your heart in it.
Anything less will kill us both.
I'm not ready to hand back my day pass.

The babbling oceans demand I give them a chance
to make good and quench my
banal thirst.
Everybody doesn't get out alive.
Can you tap-dance?
Can you juggle?
All the various worlds
claim they're the true one.
Tell them to quit kicking our asses,
we already gave,
and gave and gave and gave,
there simply isn't all that much
left to go around.

Can you bird-call?
Can you navigate?
Five seconds left on the shot clock.
Mary hails from Hell.
The bets are in.
Don't think it was anything I actually meant.
Avoid those falling civilizations,
they cause cancer and make a gentle soul
damnably vindictive.

Yes Sir, My Heart's Gonna Stay Up All Night,
Despite the Rest of Me

Don't go missing in action for too long,
I'm gonna need you for this big duet.
You feel I can hold my breath all by myself,
but since you invented oxygen
I'd kinda like you to be around
for consultation.

Everybody has a war waging in them.
Some just need to fend off skirmishes.
Some deal with major campaigns.
No confrontation is ever so insurmountable
I can't try to help you flip it over.
My own war is inconsistent.
It more often than not goes after itself,
which is okay by me,
it gives me room to try out those new
exercises you sing to me on a daily basis.

When I see you frightened and shivering in the foxhole you've imagined
so concretely for your own defensive purposes,
I get an urge to dive on in,
test those temperatures with and for you,
but sometimes your sheet music requires a reticent wood instrument
and a lot of folks claim I'm just a noisy piece of brass.

There'll be a time, though,
the old blind owl says,
when you'll step right up.
The trail ahead is often pitch-black dark.
Nobody ever got around, as of yet,
to installing the necessary lamp posts,
but you'll find your feet gracefully, fearfully moving.
Yes sirree,
your heart's gonna be up all night
despite the rest of you.

Go slow,
all the race judges are in a coma.
The warning-shot pistol is missing its firing pin.
You'll see some things.
Some things will either love or hate you.
Some things simply won't care one way or the other.
It's what it is,
nothing more.

I hear there's a cogent-enough bed-and-breakfast
perched on the ledge of a volcano
due to uncork fairly soon.
You'll get a room there,
a real bed to stretch out on.
Your favorite music will find you there.
I'll be coming over soon enough.
I'm waiting for my special order to finally come.
Don't worry too much,
the surgeons are working overtime,
doing their best to bring Earth's vital signs back.

You'll find yourself alone, once in awhile,
even if you're in the eye of the hurricane.
All those people around you
wherever you hope to go,
yet for some inexplicable reason
you feel none of them ever truly see you.
Don't fret it none.
I see you,
even when I forget how one sees.
Yes sir, my heart's
gonna stay up all your endless nights,
despite the flimsy rest of me.

A New Day Just Might Be Comin'

Come one, come all, come as you sometimes feel you are,
come lucid, come stoned, come insane, come determined,
come speaking in tongues, come screaming in silence,
a new day just might be coming.
(Maestro, if you please . . .)
Saw a lost man plant a flag in the back of a stray.
He felt it was the real deal.
The real deal folded,
got up from the table and turned into dust.
Dust is dressing up for the soirée.
The soirée is looking for its passport.
Never know when the time for escape might offer itself.

Come sloppy, come profound,
come drunk, come scary cold sober,
a new way of being seen is due any minute.
Hope you sent in the bona fide requested proper paperwork.
Hope you greased the right palms.

Come electric, come frozen,
come adept, come sunstroked,
a new way of disappearing is in the works.
Tell all concerned parties you never heard of your name.
The line forms to your something or other,
might as well call it right.
The judges for today seem half-assed cogent.
Cogent is a seaport in a tiny European country.
The fish there can't tread water.

Come stubborn, come lazy,
come in pairs,
bring your head,
make room for your heart,
a new vocabulary is trying to find the right words.
The load keeps piling on.
Doesn't a referee ever show up for work?
Somebody, who seems likable,
just handed me a code.

I can't begin to tell you what it might reveal
about the esoteric strange lack of a game plan called humanity.
Somebody told my lungs
it appreciated my intake.

Come prepared, come comatose,
come as if you mean it,
a new hope is angrily being born.
It doesn't want to leave its womb,
but Simon says get to it.
Does anybody around this immaculate dump know Simon's last name?
He left his spirit in the men's room
and there's just not so much left to say.
Maybe the chaos will only stay for a little bit.
Maybe soon it'll acquire a trade.

There's Going to Be Room Enough

There's this room with your name on it
at the end of some road that claims it's a hall.
There's this room waiting for you to call it home.
There's going to be more than enough room for you in it.

The furniture might move around on its own accord,
the bed might deny you a good night's rest
every now and then,
but nobody can forcibly evict you from it.

This room goes by many different names.
It keeps altering its outlook.
Don't get frustrated, friend,
this still is the best damn room in town.
The rates remain practically human.

Sometimes you want to close the window
so the cold won't get in.
Sometimes the window don't budge.
That window sure has an ego.
Sometimes you can't take the humidity.
Just don't declare war on the heat.

This room will eventually learn to love you
for who you actually are.
If you try to be someone you never are
this room will turn on you.

There's this room that's going to love you.
Doesn't matter if you sometimes feel you can't be loved.
This room is going to let you in it
even if the key breaks in the lock.

There's going to be room enough in this room.
You'll be able to dance.
I know you once wrote a series of best-selling books
swearing you didn't know how to dance,
but the room never finished any of them.

It reads your skin and heart instead.

The room knows you're en route.
The journey might last a bit longer.
It does get to be that way
now and then.
Keep your head up,
eyes open.

The road might snap at your heels
but its bark is more dramatic than its actual bite.
The desk clerk
sometimes can be found
standing by,
ready and willing to offer help
if needed.

This room goes by many names
but truly responds to only one.
It's the one name your heart
paints it.
I know you once told your biographers
that your heart was incapable of flying.
This morning I saw it somersaulting in the sky.

No Water Gets Out Alive

Claim no superiority before its time.
Speak to mud with conviction.
We all were stumps once,
by the side of the road.
Our branches claim they know the territory.
Reach now and pull the plug.
Time to drain it all down.
No water gets out alive.

The main argument is hollow.
Children live inside it.
Come upstairs and feed something.
I want to belong to anyone who needs.
Can't walk all directions at once.
Talk slow, I can't hear what you see.

Claim claim claim no judgment before its time.
The mud speaks of you with conviction.
I am stumped
by the side of any road.
My branch knows no territory.
Reach now, reach and be electric.
The water, it raises its hand.
I intend to become alive.

All of the little arguments want to be mountains.
Old men hide out in them.
Come upstairs and be fed upon.
I want to need anyone who can belong.
All directions at once walk on me.
Hear it slow, I can't smell what you touch.
They've asked us to coordinate the dance.
Yes yes yes, I feel I can fly that route.
I, born of mud,
am convinced.

When Speechlessness Gets Too Loud

I'm gonna do one more.
I'll take requests.
The ambulances are all tucked in for the night.
The shrapnel in our hearts is all blessed.
Give me just one second to set my bearings.
The war just took a piss on the White House lawn.
Naughty, naughty.
Will this class be pass or fail?
Is the teacher any good?
His ex-students walk funny.
Why am I always so hungry?
Something in the telling of the tail of the tale.

I'm gonna sing one last time.
I don't know the words.
It never stopped me before.
Turn your face toward the last drop of water.
Take a drink for me.
Sometimes the speechlessness
gets too loud.
Brokedown humans
still demand your respect.
The cab meter runs
and the crazies live in the banks.

I'm gonna shoot you a three-pointer,
then I think they want me gone.
They mumble so well when they talk,
I never know.
The young maidens fall from the state-sponsored sky.
Lots of poison still going around.
The FDA moves slow.
Give me a slice.
Why would I worry?
All nights have middles.
Being in them
does not hurt.
Swim this way.

Caress all tears.
The war room only has one key.
I
just
swallowed
it.